FELISHA UPSHAW

COLLEGE NEWBIES

GET ADVICE
BEFORE
STEPPING
ON CAMPUS

College Newbies: Get advice before stepping on campus / Felisha Upshaw

ISBN-13: 978-0692693889
ISBN-10: 0692693882

My Time Publishing
Memphis, Tennessee

1. College Reference —Self-Help
First Edition

CONTENTS

ACKNOWLEDGEMENTS

I'd like to thank God for placing it upon my heart to write this book.

To my mother, Birdie Upshaw, thank you for always believing in me, supporting me and praying for me.

I would like to thank my good friend, Patricia Martin for her encouragement throughout this process.

To the students I've encountered, I appreciate each of you for sharing your fears and future goals with me.

Lastly but certainly not least, thanks to those of you who have taken interest in this book. Every aspect was written keeping our incoming freshman in mind. Thank you.

If you take nothing else from this book, take this:

You can make it through any obstacle that falls in
your path, just keep going and never give up.

INTRODUCTION

Many incoming freshmen are plagued by several unsettling questions:

- "Will I make any friends?"
- "Is the class work difficult?"
- "What major should I choose?"
- "Which college should I attend?"
- "How will I pay for tuition?"

There is no doubt, you will have lots of questions and it is okay if you're unable to answer them right away. Don't panic, just calm down and breathe. Take each question and write them on paper. Tackle the easy ones first, and then move to those that are more complex.

Are you nervous about college? Do you have butterflies in your stomach?

That's normal.

Don't be frightened, most of the incoming freshmen feel the same way you do. College is about overcoming fears, such as the one you're feeling right now. It is also about creating memories, learning, growing, laughing and having fun.

This book will calm those butterflies.

We will look at every common question and provide the best possible advice to heighten your confidence in approaching college. You'll learn how to socialize with peers and professors, face academic challenges and save money.

I've had my share of college experiences, from commuting to staying on campus, from changing colleges to changing majors. I went from a C student to an A student. Well, of course, I scored a couple of (Bs) as well but that's great too, right?

Transitioning into college unguided was one of the biggest mistakes I made. I want to encourage you to seek guidance. Sure, people will throw advice but how much of it actually sticks, especially if it's coming quick from so many people.

I depended on the high school counselor for advice and she failed me. Basically, telling me I couldn't accomplish my goal. She judged me by where I was that day instead of who I had the potential to become.

During my college years, I created a website dedicated to giving college freshmen information and advice (www.collegenewbies.com). After graduating college, I begin mentoring students in the community, helping high school student's transition into college freshman. This book allows me to reach more students to inform, encourage and support.

In the end, my college experience was priceless. I learned the true meaning of independence. I learned to make decisions for myself and navigate through an unfamiliar town. I chose my own classes and figured out the financial aspects at an early age.

The learning process is a growing process. It's the experiences we go through that teach us to become better. By the time I completed college, I had experienced a great number of ups and downs. Incoming freshman should not face this transition alone. Sincere help should always be available.

Advice will be shared throughout this book, in the hope that you will not take a prolonged route to reach your goal. Now, let's take a quick peep at the next section *Plan Your Future* before moving further into the book.

PLAN YOUR FUTURE

Students, you've done an amazing job graduating high school. You have pushed through one of the most important phases of your life. College is the next important step. It provides opportunities to set goals without any boundaries. College can be a gateway to freedom but the question is, "Are you ready to face new challenges that go along with that freedom?"

If you've selected this book, there is a good chance you are ready.

College planning is the best way to begin your journey and with any journey, you need a guide. Think of this book as your guide.

Why do you need a plan for college anyway?

Well, answer this question, why turn on the lights before walking into a dark room? To see where you're going, right? Yes. So, grab a pen and notebook to write down your vision before heading to college.

Choosing not to turn on the lights before walking into a dark room, automatically places obstacles in the way. Think of your college plans the same way and remove any foreseen problems.

Let's say your plan is to become a nurse. Your next move is to select a college with this program of study. Request a catalog from the selected college. Talk with the college advisor to let them know your interests. Look at the requirements for nursing and the number of years it takes to complete the degree.

It's always a great idea to know the direction you will take. In fact, in your notebook, interrogate yourself with questions:

- What do I wish to gain from college?
- What is the expected salary amount for my chosen major?
- Who do I want to become in college?
- Will I study abroad?
- What type of experiences do I want from college?

Write down things you want from college and figure out how to get them. The idea may not appear necessary now but when you have a plan, there is a better chance you will succeed.

Note: Avoid drifting through college, guide your destiny.

A NOTE TO STUDENTS

Students, I would like to tell you that everyone who attends college can become a successful individual or an entrepreneur with a luxury lifestyle, however it doesn't always work that way. College alone, can't guarantee wealth or satisfaction but it gives you an advantage. The exciting part is knowing you have control on which steps you will take. At this point, you're doing great. You've graduated high school, decided to attend college and selected this book as your college guide. If you continue making great decisions, college success will be your next major step.

Many people have already been where you are and most of us wish we could start over and correct our past mistakes. We look back and say, "I wish I would have pursued that." I want you to become the person that looks back and say, "I am content with where I am today."

Sometimes we get stuck in our dreams, instead of making them a reality. To make those dreams of being a college graduate come true, face reality which is going to college with the intention of leaving with a degree.

Afterwards, you will be on a higher level with more options of employment, salary and positions. It will not be an easy journey but it can be done with self-motivation, hard work, commitment and firm guidance.

You are the best asset for your future and only you can make great things happen in your life, not mom or dad. Of course, they are a huge support team through it all but you are the person who has to physically and mentally create your future by getting involved in coursework, activities, socializing and studying.

The time is now to take control over your future and become independent young adults. Your life will be everything you want it to be and more if you make the right choices in the beginning.

Does this mean every choice will be the best? Certainly not, we are human and as humans we will make mistakes. Yet, our mistakes give us experience to learn and grow, creating a promising future.

At this point, the high school you attended, the city you're from or your popularity is not as relevant as it was in high school. Those things are not relevant as they once were because you will meet new people who are not aware of your past. There will be new faces, new instructors and a completely different environment. This is the commencement, which means the beginning for you. This is the stage in your life where you decide who you want to be and create that life for yourself. You're preparing for your future and getting an education that no one can take from you. You can find joy in knowing that it was you who took those classes, made it to class on time and received those good scores to earn a degree in your chosen field.

Completing any major and receiving a degree, demonstrates that you are dedicated and capable of finishing projects. College does not discriminate against who can and cannot receive an education. This opportunity is open to anyone who believes in his or herself to get the job done. Any career that you're holding in your heart and mind, do it.

Remove any self-doubt and fear, go for it. You never know what capabilities you possess unless you push yourself. Oh yes, don't forget to have fun in the process.

MY REASONS FOR ATTENDING COLLEGE:

Before we continue, write your five reasons for attending college. Anytime you get discouraged through this journey. Refer to this page.

1.
_____

_____

2.
_____

_____

3.
_____

_____

4.
_____

_____

5.
_____

PART 1

PREPPING
FOR COLLEGE

REGISTRATION READY

Stepping away from the long line, Kara finally approached the administrator's desk. She was missing needed paperwork; they advised her to come back when her high school transcript had been submitted. Kara seemed irritated after learning much time had been wasted; only to be turned away.

Registering for college seems simple, right? You send the proper paperwork, choose a few classes, pay for college expenses and you're done. Supposedly, that's how it works. As a newcomer, the process can seem tedious; making it possible to miss a step. I decided to insert this section for that young lady and all other incoming freshman.

On registration day, clear your schedule as the process can be time consuming. Be aware that there may be a lot of walking from admissions to financial aid and other areas on campus. To make this process smooth as possible, send all required documents to the college prior to your arrival such as high school transcript, application for admission and ACT/SAT scores. Also, fill out a FAFSA (Free Application for

Federal Student Aid) application before the deadline. This helps at registration to know if you qualify or not for assistance.

This chart is what you will see on the FAFSA website: Please see below deadlines.

Aid Program	Deadline Information
Federal student aid	Please visit www.fafsa.com for the year you will be attending.
	There are a few *federal student aid programs* that have limited funds, so be sure to apply as soon as you can once the FAFSA is available for the year you'll be attending school.
State student aid	You can find state deadlines at fafsa.gov or on the paper or PDF FAFSA. Note that several states have financial aid programs with limited funds and therefore have a deadline of "as soon as possible (after the FAFSA becomes available)."
College or career school aid	Check the school's website or contact its *financial aid office*. School deadlines are usually early in the year (often in February or March, although some may be even earlier now that the FAFSA is available in October).

Other financial aid	Some programs other than government or school aid require that you file the FAFSA. For instance, you can't get certain private scholarships unless you're eligible for a Federal Pell Grant—and you can't find out whether you're eligible for a Pell Grant unless you file a FAFSA. If the private scholarship's application deadline is in early to mid-January, you'll need to submit your FAFSA before that deadline.

The financial aid administrator will advise if you're granted financial aid and inform on the amount you will receive. If the application has not been completely processed, the administrator will inform you to follow up later. If you're like me, you want to know the amount you're receiving soon as possible. So, it is best to complete FAFSA in advance. If you are not granted financial aid, you will pay for tuition and fees upon registration.

Send any other important paperwork needed to complete the registration process. Check the college website for specific information or call in advance to know exactly what items are needed.

Another check-off on your list of things to do is mail-in housing applications. Send housing applications early to avoid being on the waiting list. The last thing you need is classes to start and you're unable to attend because no dorm rooms are available. When I was in college this happened to a student I knew. She mailed the application for a dorm room near the start date of college. Classes began and Chasity did not have a room, luckily, she had family in the area that assisted with temporary housing. If she hadn't had family in that area, she would have been forced to commute until a dorm became available.

Now, the important papers are sent.

The next important step is to choose classes prior to your arrival (This is optional-but it helps). Request a college catalog or check the catalog online to see your required courses. View the required courses for your program of study and select the classes you wish to take. Also, decide if you will be a full-time student or part-time student. Full-time students are enrolled in 12 credit hours (4 classes) or more. 12 credit hours or less is considered a part-time student.

Will you enroll as a full-time or part-time student?

Let's pick an available start time for the course. There will be a variety of times through-out the day in which you could choose. *Mornings, evenings* or *night* classes are offered. *Morning* is a great time to learn when your mind is clear of everything. This is when you have the most energy. You also have time remaining in the day to visit the library or somewhere of your choice. If you are one of those students who struggle to awake early mornings, it would not be a good idea to schedule early classes (7:00 or 8:00 am). Perhaps, you could enroll in later morning courses like 10:00 or 11:00am. The *evening* classes would be ideal to avoid missing any classes. You can sleep later without the interruption of an alarm clock and attend classes well-rested and alert. The *night* classes are the third option, typically, they are longer than morning and evening courses but night classes are great if you have a day-time job or other responsibilities.

Next, choose the days you would like to attend such as Monday, Wednesday and Friday (MWF) or Tuesdays and Thursdays (TR). Decide the best time for you to learn and choose which best fits your schedule. Selecting classes, days and time before arriving on campus, solely depends on the school you choose. You may or may not be able to do so. The idea is to have choices prior to seeing your college advisor. The counselor will meet with you to select courses and ensure you are taking all required classes for your major. It's always a good idea to be knowledgeable about the process, relating to selecting courses and understanding your course requirements. Why? You don't want to be delayed for graduation because your advisor failed to mention a class. It's better if you two work together.

When registering for classes, ensure you are comfortable with the chosen courses. It's not a good idea to take more than one class that you find difficult. For example, if calculus and biology in one semester is too much, inform your advisor about the matter. It may be possible to take one of those classes, the following semester. (Classes are broken down into semesters by the college) Again, each college will have different rules. The earlier you get to the college for registration, the better your chances are of getting the classes you want.

Certain majors require students to pass a test, make certain scores on the ACT or take prerequisite courses prior to admission. For example, special programs such as respiratory therapy or nursing. For many other students, placement test is given and used to assess college readiness, placing students into their appropriate class levels. All this information should be known in advance to decrease any confusion.

Tip: If you didn't do so at an orientation session, take a tour of the campus during registration. In the mix of registering, talk to other students to make connections, when you see them again, you could say hello and chat to possibly become friends or acquaintances.

Note: The downside to not having a dorm, leads to students missing class. This is when the accumulation of absences begins. Of course, exceeding your absences without officially dropping the class is the quickest way to be withdrawn from the course and receive an F. You must officially withdraw from the class and receive a W (withdraw). Although, you are accepted into the college and have registered for classes, you must be certain you have a dorm room as well.

Checklist: Did you mail all required admissions paperwork? Did you mail the housing application for a room assignment? Have you pre-selected courses before going to the campus? Have you cleared your schedule for registration day? Will you enroll as a full-time or part-time student? Are you a morning, evening or night person?

SCHOLARSHIPS

Let's talk about free money. To many students, scholarships seem to be non-existent however they are available. It just takes a little time and research to find them.

What are scholarships anyway?

A scholarship is financial aid or a grant provided to a student for academic merit and various other reasons so that he or she can continue their education. Scholarships are a great help, they don't need to be repaid.

There are several categories for scholarships and they are awarded depending on different criteria. Research and apply for those that fit your status. Take advantage of any money given to you for free. No matter how small the amount, it will be helpful for college expenses.

Check with your previous high school counselor and your new college advisor to know what options are available to receive scholarships. Local career centers offer grants (depends on the state you reside). Local libraries will have updated books on scholarships. There are several sources in book stores, dedicated to scholarship information. If you're currently employed, check with human resources; they may offer tuition assistance. FedEx is one of the many companies offering tuition assistance to their employees. There are also scholarships only a small percentage of people know about. For example, if you are left-handed, you could receive a scholarship. How cool is that? Tennessee offers free community college to all state residents, regardless of merit or need. This scholarship is called the Tennessee Promise. Of course, there are stipulations. Applying for scholarships is free, if someone is requesting money, it's likely to be a scam.

HOMESICK

In the beginning of college, it can be difficult adjusting into your new environment. Many students begin to miss family, their own space, privacy and mother's delicious home-cooked meals or simply watching sports with dad. At times, you may feel abandoned by family or others but keep going and understand that no one has forgotten you. They may be occupied with other tasks.

Socialize with peers, join clubs and enjoy the many activities on campus; later, home will not be a major concern. The more you enjoy the college life, the less you will travel home. Your trip home every weekend will eventually become a trip home every other weekend. Granted, you're within a short distance from home. This is when you know you're officially over being homesick. Stay busy as it occupies your mind, it keeps you from thinking about home. Call family during lonely times. Reach out to family/friends through face time, Skype or any social networks. Bring items from home like family pictures. Eventually, you will get comfortable in your new setting and everything will get better.

ITEMS NEEDED FOR COLLEGE

Let's do a quick check-off for needed items:

- Toothbrush/ toothpaste
- Mouthwash
- Shower Caddy
- Comforter/ twin bed sheets/pillows
- Disinfectant wipes/spray
- Shower shoes
- Shower caps
- House shoes/slippers
- Soap
- Entertainment (book, music, Xbox)
- Broom/dust pan
- Pajamas
- Laptop
- Umbrella
- Snacks
- Small refrigerator (Check w/roommate)
- Small T.V (Check w/Roommate)
- Car charger/portable charger

- Reusable water bottle
- Alarm clock/phone clock
- Ear buds for phone
- Feminine products
- 3 Ring Binder
- Post It Notes (Optional)
- Spiral Notebook
- Pens
- Highlighters
- Scissors
- Tape
- Bathrobe
- Clothes hangers
- Towels
- Mattress pad (your choice)
- Laundry Supplies
- Postage Stamps
- Tissue
- Medications and first aid items
- Surge protector
- Coaxial cable for the TV

PART 2

CHOOSING A MAJOR

EVALUATE YOUR CAREER INTEREST AND GO FOR IT

It was senior year in high school and the teacher had begun sending students to the counselor's office, one-by-one.

"Felisha Upshaw, your turn to see the counselor," the teacher said with a smile.

I was excited, it would be the first time talking with someone about my college plans. Of course, my family was excited about me attending college but they didn't advise on the steps I should take. As I sat in front of the counselor's desk, she begins discussing my future plans.

"What do you want to major in when you attend college?" she asked.

"A physical therapist," I said.

"Maybe you should try physical therapy assistant."

My heart dropped as I sat there in silence, totally confused.

After that statement, the counseling session was (mentally) over for me. I couldn't understand her suggestion of physical therapy assistant instead of an actual physical therapist. Later that day, I figured since my grades were border line (Cs category), she didn't think I was smart enough.

During that time in my life, I was my worst critic and didn't need any help. I was discouraged immediately. I began having second thoughts about majoring in physical therapy. I begin thinking maybe I'm not smart enough to pursue that career. I explained the situation to my allied health teacher and I believe she was more upset than I was. She told me I could become whatever I wanted and never let anyone tell me different.

Today, I am still grateful for those words of encouragement from Mrs. Zinn. I'm not a physical therapist today, not because someone told me I couldn't do it but because I chose to follow a different career path.

When choosing your major, do not allow anyone to make you think your goals cannot be achieved. You can challenge any career that interest you, don't worry about your high school grades because what you have at that point cannot be changed. Low or average grades do not define your success. Your ability to overcome past performances and strive for higher scores will allow you to succeed in college.

When deciding on a major, think about something you are skilled in or have a passion about, maybe even a talent. Choose a career you will be content doing every day.

Why should you do this?

Enjoying your job will have a positive impact in your life by getting paid to do what you enjoy versus disliking your career and stressing about it each day. For example, if you chose to be a coach because you love sports, you will enjoy the topics that will be discussed in class. You will look forward to attending class and be more active in the course. After graduating from that major and becoming employed, it will be easy adjusting into your career field. On the other hand, choosing a career because it pays well or it sounds good like a veterinarian but you dislike animals, you may not enjoy the classes being taught or you may lack motivation and possibly dislike your job.

The point is to actually think about a fulfilling major you want as a career. If you are not sure what you're skilled in or don't know what you enjoy doing? That's okay, no one expects you to have it all figured out just yet.

Try self-evaluating questions such as, "am I a great communicator or do I enjoy talking?" If you said yes, major in communications, broadcasting journalism, speech pathologist or anything similar. If you like designing websites, coding or removing viruses from computers for a hobby, pursue a career in the computer field of study. Are you interested in how others think, act or behave? Psychology is the way to go. What is your favorite academic subject? Do you prefer simple and complex equations (math), maybe you're into rearranging sentences and spelling every word correct (English)? You could possibly love the facts of past events (history). Turn one of those favorite subjects into a profession such as a high school teacher or a professor at a university.

Are you still not sure?

No problem, let's continue analyzing your qualities.

Do you like to cook? If so, think about culinary arts, how does master chef sound? Love caring for others? Maybe nursing is for you. What can you do well? Think about things others say you do well.

There are many more professions to choose from, write down a list of careers that may be of interest to you and from there create a pros and cons list of each career. Do not underestimate yourself when listing these careers. Write down any major you would enjoy pursuing. Go back and eliminate those that do not hold your interest. Research each major, check the standard hours, salary and all other information that may be of importance to you. Check your major's course description in the college catalog. This will give an overview about each class you pursue. It would be a great idea to rent and/or buy a DVD, watch YouTube videos or stop by the local library to get details on different careers to gain understanding of what the job entitles.

When you finally decide on a career, talk to someone with the same title as your chosen career. If possible, shadow them at their job to be certain that's what you want to do. Ask him or her questions about their career:

- *Do you like your job?*
- *How many years have you been employed in this career?*
- *What are the advantages and disadvantages of being in this field of study?*

Anything that comes to mind, simply ask.

Interview more than one person to get different insights. Each person will have a different view that could be helpful. In the process of doing this, do not allow anyone to alter your career decision. Get the facts but follow your heart and make your own decisions.

Picking a career takes careful thought and lots of time but is well worth the effort and research. The more you learn about the major, the more you will wish to pursue it or decide against it. Your interest or passion may change over time. The general idea is to pick a major, creating a plan you can work toward. Think about the career and choose wisely. In addition to choosing a major you can identify with, choose an occupation that is in high demand. Read the next section on demanding jobs.

Checklist questions: What can you do well? Can you imagine doing this job every day? Name six careers that interest you the most. Jot down the pros and cons of each career. Write the salary amount beside each career listed.

HIGH AND LOW
DEMAND CAREERS

Philip Hayes, a teenager from Texas, grew up in the country fields. He was very interested in cropping and farming. Watching the neighbors on his street take care of their land, Philip was certain that was the path he should take. He decided to study agricultural engineering at the University of Georgia.

While completing his senior year, he sent resumes to different companies and played the waiting game. Months passed, interviews were done and a constant search for employment continued but there was no luck. It was unfortunate Philip's career was not in high demand; it pushed him to work in town until he could find employment in his career field. (According to bls.gov) Agricultural engineering has a slower than average job growth through 2024.

Situations like these can be decreased by doing research before choosing a major. Selecting a high demand career increases the chances of employment after graduation.

Students, you will juggle many tasks while transitioning

into college and seldom think to research the demand of your chosen major. However, research should be on the priority list.

Imagine studying a major for two to four years only to graduate and not get a job. It's a waste of time, right? So, why not take a moment to (research) Google 'high demanding careers' prior to college. This does not guarantee employment after graduation but it does increase your chances.

What is a high demand career exactly? Well, it is basically a job that employers seek the most and while you may commonly see doctors and nurses in high demand, there are also other popular careers to consider. A market research analyst is a good example; they have a much faster than average job growth through the year 2022. The job growth for computer and mathematical occupations such as software developers and accountants are also growing faster than average. Keep in mind, the higher career demand, the more people are needed to fill positions, which means a better chance to snatch and keep a job.

So, if you choose a major that is in high demand with a fast growth potential, kudos to you for making the right choice. A demanding career also provides opportunities for relocation to other states, considering the employment growth for the chosen career field (in that state).

Let's say you are a dentist and you moved from your

hometown to Colorado, there is a great chance you will find employment since your career has a high demand rate. On the other hand, if a major is not in high demand, finding employment could be difficult. The low demanding careers will not fill as many positions, which lead to difficulty in finding employment. Also, other students and job seekers with years of experience will be applying for these low demand careers, which makes it even more competitive and a slim chance for newcomers.

It's best to work hard and obtain knowledge that could place you in a better position. Learn as much information about the career as possible. Employers want to know if you would be an asset to their company and if given the opportunity, could you match physical skills with your mental skills. Research your major to confirm it's at the top of the charts for job growth. Refer to the occupational outlook handbook or online for more details. It offers helpful data on employment growth, salary and details about various occupations.

Your job throughout college is to do your absolute best to be in the top percentage of students and it would not hurt to study a major that is in high demand. After learning this information, is your major high or low in demand? (Reference bls.gov)

Checklist: Make a list of high demand careers that are interesting to you.

CHECK WEB SITES
FOR JOBS

Once you've selected your major, check web sites for jobs pertaining to the major. Why should you do this? To see the number of positions available in your hometown or the city you choose to reside. Check how often jobs are available. Search the websites periodically to get an idea of what employers are expecting from their employees. View the requirements and salary the employers offer. Also, view the description of the job and all it entitles.

Knowing what employers are seeking helps you in selecting courses throughout college. For example, if you are a computer major and jobs in the area are searching for someone to troubleshoot, perform maintenance on computers and so on. You would take classes that teach these things, making you more qualified for the position. Check the description of the class in your college catalog. Also, view the turnover rate for the potential employer. Turnover rate means to replace an employee with a new employee. A high turnover rate could mean employees are unhappy with their job and decided to quit. It could also mean employers have many lay-offs that cause the high rates. There could be several reasons the employers are having a high turnover rate. On the other hand, a low turnover rate means employees are satisfied with their jobs and employers are not having major issues with the staff. Checking websites for jobs allow you to get insight on your chosen career.

EXPECTED INCOME FOR YOUR CAREER STUDENT LOAN

After graduation, many students find themselves in debt with college loans. While there is no simple or easy way to graduate debt free, some students could decrease the amount with the correct financial planning. Luckily, you will be planning ahead to provide better results for your finances and education.

How will this be accomplished?

First, write down these many questions.

- What is your major?
- What is the tuition for this major?
- How much does your chosen major average a year?
- Will the expected income from your career be enough money to re-pay student loans and live your personal life comfortably?
- Who will fund your educational expenses?
- What is their limit?
- Will you assist with these costs?

- What other financial responsibilities do you have at this point?
- What loan amount will place you in debt?

Include parents or those funding your education.

Allow these questions to marinate in your mind before making a huge commitment to any loan agreements. After analyzing all questions, there should be a better view on where to begin with your education and expenses. Choose a career that will have a balance of financial growth and contentment. After all, you are investing money and time.

If you cringe at the sound of people talking about student loans or even feel burdened by the pressures of student loans? Don't worry, since you are a genius, you have already discussed finances with your parents or support team. They will take care of those financial obligations, while you focus on picking a major with an acceptable salary amount. Ensure you will receive a great amount of income after college to help re-pay student loans and stabilize your day to day living.

First, get an understanding about the salary of your career choice. How much will your career average a year? Students seldom check their major's expected income but the salary for the year or hourly pay for your chosen occupation should be researched.

Why?

To get an idea of the amount of money that will be earned and to know the lifestyle you can afford with that salary. Think about this, some majors average $23,000 to $30,000 a year. This amount can be earned at businesses without any college degree. So, why not aim higher in terms of salary by choosing a major with a higher income? Of course, money should not be the only focus but being comfortable with finances are important.

A lot of time should be taken on financial decisions versus any other college decision. To be even more clear about the idea. Look at your parents' current living status. Do your parents struggle to make payments on utilities? Or have they effortlessly taken care of bills and indulged in a few vacations on the side. Maybe they're somewhere in between by taking care of the house but unable to take trips out of town. You be the judge. Take this information and decide which of the three situations best fits you. This is not to pass judgment on your parents; they provide with love, regardless of their salary amount. This is only to assess your current living status and compare to what you desire in the future.

Now that we have an understanding about career income, let's look at student loans. Student loans are known to be a real pain for college students. After graduation, you are given six months to find employment before re-paying college loans. So, it's best to choose a major earning more or close to your loan amount. This way you're able to re-pay loans without financial hardship. Otherwise, it will be difficult and frustrating to owe thousands of dollars when you're not averaging enough money to repay the loan. Although, loans do not have to be repaid in one lump sum, a great amount will be subtracted from your paycheck for many years. If student loans are not repaid when required, interest will be added, which makes the situation worse. Attending college for years only to graduate and be in debt for a long period of your life will become stressful.

How much will you borrow for student loans? Remember, it is suggested to only borrow what is needed for tuition. Also, be mindful that borrowing loans for reasons other than educational purposes may be a huge mistake. While the idea sounds tempting and the resources are available, any mistakes will be a barrier in your future if not given any careful thought. Employed or not, it's mandatory that loans are repaid after college.

A pen and notebook will be essential to write down the amount of your major's tuition, books and all other fees. College tuition will be different from public to private and online colleges. Borrow that specific amount and go from there. Always research and ask many questions, get counseling from parents, former high school teachers or anyone knowledgeable and trustworthy to assist you before borrowing money for college. Calculate the cost before taking out loans for any career. If you're unclear about interest rates on loans, familiarize yourself with this information or speak with a financial aid administrator. You could also stop by a bank; they would be happy to explain how interest rates work. Students, be aware of college debt, however do not allow it to stop you from achieving your career goals. View it as an investment that will provide opportunities.

Note: If financial aid covers the entire tuition, which is possible, a major you desire with a low-income amount may be acceptable for a career. Who knows, you could possibly get promoted within the company to earn a higher salary.

Checklist: Name those who will assist with college expenses. What is the salary for the major? Is the salary acceptable? Is the major worth the loan amount accumulated? How much income do you wish to make?

CHANGING MAJORS CHALLENGING COURSES COMPLETING THE MAJOR

CHANGING MAJORS

"I want to be a teacher," "I want be a nurse," "I want to be a lawyer"—these famous lines are common among students exiting high school. They are great careers however problems arise after the first semester; students begin to contemplate their next major.

Changing major's will cross your mind once or twice, maybe even three times and it's perfectly normal however it is not something you want to do consistently. Constantly changing majors will affect you for many reasons. *First reason*, it prolongs completing required courses to receive the degree in a timely manner. What does that mean? Well, it means you may attend a community college for two years or longer, not making any progress toward graduating or you may attend a university for four years or longer without getting any results.

The *second reason* to avoid changing majors is taking classes you don't need. For example, if you've taken three classes in criminal justice and later transition into computer science, what just happened? You've prolonged graduation and used unnecessary money on courses you didn't need. Be mindful, these classes are expensive, wasting time is wasting money. In addition to that, it's possible to get burned out from taking various courses that are not required for your chosen career field.

Another reason to avoid taking classes you don't need is encountering difficult classes that sometimes lead to failing scores. Guess what happens when you make failing scores? It lowers your GPA. The U.S Department of Education does not grant money to students with failing grades. In situations, such as this, you will need to file an appeal to continue receiving assistance, so let's avoid these problems.

One *last reason* to avoid changing majors is the accumulation of too many credits. In many community colleges, financial aid will not be granted after exceeding the required amount of credits. Reference your college catalog or speak with a college advisor on this matter.

The objective is to focus on your chosen major and stick with it until the end. I'm not saying never change majors but be certain about any changes you make. On the flip side, if you find yourself interested in two careers and unable to decide. There is the option to have a major and minor. The major will be the primary focus. The minor is your secondary interest. If you decide to switch the minor to major, some of the classes will already be completed. To lessen the number of times you change majors, take the required general courses in the first semester and perhaps, the following semester too. Time will not be wasted in taking this route because these classes will be requirements at some point.

Note: Several students who are undecided on a major, generally feels pressured to pick one. They automatically choose a career that would earn lots of money, without putting any thought behind the career itself. Sometimes students choose a major because someone else (parents, counselors) advised it, learning later, the career is not what he or she would like to do.

Be careful choosing a major because someone else advised it. You will be the person physically performing the job every day, so it's only fair you make that decision. Many others have said, "You don't have to rush to select a career." This is true but also keep in mind, college tuition is often increasing. Picking a major should be done as quickly as possible. Remember, whatever you decide, be sure it's a decision you are making on your own. Follow your dreams, and choose your path.

CHALLENGING COURSES

There will be this temptation to change majors due to difficult courses. The first and most important rule for difficult classes is to face them, do not give up. Exhaust all methods prior to changing a major due to challenging courses.

What are the methods? Glad you asked, use the (3T) method which is Tutors, Time and Teachers.

Tutors are simply your private instructor. When you're one on one with the tutor, ask questions about any and everything you don't understand, their job is to break down the assignment or topic for clear understanding. Many campuses offer free tutoring lessons, check with administrators for information.

Time is the next method and it must be invested into your education, take time to study. This means turn off everything that distracts from studying such as the phone, television and avoid friends, unless they are studying with you. In fact, the best place to study is the library in peace and quiet, sit near a corner and face the wall to refrain from looking up at everyone walking by.

It's understood that you are no kid and this is not time-out, it may even sound a little strange but the objective is to focus. I understand this is easier said than done. While you're studying, try not to think about what your friends are doing at the mall. Just ask yourself, how will being at the mall help you pass a test?

The third option, last but certainly not least is *teachers*. They will figure out the solution to your difficulties, they review your low test scores, class assignments and/or home work. They are there to help you learn the material, if you have any questions, feel free to ask. Set up appointments to meet with them about your progress in class. After taken these steps there is a great chance you will excel in those classes.

Note: Make sure you never give up on something you want. Everyone goes through difficult times but we must be persistent to have a great outcome.

COMPLETING THE MAJOR

After identifying your major and getting beyond challenging courses, continue and complete the major immediately. Why should you do this? You are young and have the advantage of living on campus without feeling out of place. You have very little, if any, financial responsibilities. Coursework is fresh in your memory, and not many worries. Your brain and body is familiar with the speed you're going, so what is stopping you from continuing your education immediately?

You should let nothing or no one put a pause on your goals, not even yourself. Let's say you took a break for a few years and now you wish to return to college. At this point, you are employed with a decent job that you are content and comfortable performing. Although it's not the career job you desire, you refuse to leave because the pay is acceptable to your living status.

You're working and attending college, which is more difficult to dedicate 100% to your studies, now the workload has doubled. Let's also imagine you've started a family, now you must provide for your family which makes the situation even more complex. At this point, you have a job, family and school that must be balanced.

There are so many things that could happen within those few years of your life. People that start their education later in life, sometimes get comfortable in the current position. They make excuses for not continuing their education. They say, "I will go back when the child is in school" or "I will go back this semester, next semester." Eventually another few years have passed and they stop thinking about it. Starting college and finishing college is best when completed in the earliest part of your life which is directly from high school. Well, of course, after a summer break.

Checklist questions: Why are you changing your major? What is your strategy to tackle difficult courses? What is the plan to complete your major?

PART 3

UNCOMMON CAREER IDEAS

The following careers are uncommon for students to pick; however, the earning potential is good.

POLITICS

If you have political plans following college, be sure you have researched the requirements. Many politicians study economics, law, business, political science or international relations. Include communication courses as they are helpful with public speaking. A college degree is not required however people are very careful with the leaders they choose. So, do you think obtaining a degree is a smart choice? I'd vote yes. Also, keep a clean background.

PROFESSIONAL TRUCK DRIVER

Have you ever dreamed of traveling the world? Becoming a truck driver would be a great chance to do so. You don't need a college degree however obtaining a career certificate or weeks of training will be required. Professional truck drivers sometimes become an entrepreneur by owning his or her own freight company. If you decide to take this path, you may wish to take courses to get knowledge in customs brokerage, transportation, or even business. This is not necessary but it would be helpful for you to understand the business you plan to build. It increases your knowledge, helping you to become a successful truck driver or owner.

There are different routes you could take with this career. You could land a job in a transportation facility or college, training other students. A college degree may be required for hire at colleges. You could also start your own training facility; teaching students how to drive an eighteen-wheeler.

Note: If possible, receive training from colleges rather than sponsored CDL training programs. The cost is cheaper.

PUBLIC SPEAKING

Public speaking can be promising to those who know how to articulate words and speak with confidence. Public speaking can be very useful in such a loud world of individuals. If you are looking to become a sales person for a company or perhaps a recruiter, life coach or motivational speaker; public speaking will fit you well. Tony Robbins and Les Brown are great examples of speakers whom have taken their careers to high levels. The earning potential depends on the area of expertise you delve into. While public speaking is mentioned as an uncommon career; a communications degree is what leads students into this field of study.

REAL ESTATE

Looking to become the mastermind in real estate? No problem—as a professional real estate agent, you will certainly need a marketing degree and within that degree be sure economics and finance are classes you are enrolled into. These professionals buy, sell, and rent properties for their clients. They tend to have a personality that enjoys networking and fulfilling the needs of others. Per bls.gov, real estate occupations (agents, brokers, managers) salary ranged from $58,410 to $68,240. Real estate appears to be an interesting career to research.

There are many more uncommon career ideas to explore. Further your search to notice which ones you would love to pursue.

PART 4

CHOOSING
A COLLEGE

COMMUNITY COLLEGE OR UNIVERSITY

Community colleges and universities will grant access to degrees, social life, fun and possibilities. The only thing you must do is choose which of the two is best for you. It would be beneficial to compare community colleges and universities prior to deciding.

Write down a list of benefits of both a community college and university, starting from the most important benefits to the least important.

Let's view the community college first. Now, while a community college would be recommended to jump start your education. Many people overlook and sometimes downplay community college however great careers can be obtained from a two-year institution. For example, nurses, dental hygienist, and funeral service occupations can be earned at the community college with an earning potential of $50,000 or greater.

Community colleges offer opportunities to earn associate degrees and career certificates at an affordable amount. They have smaller class sizes, which allow the professor to become familiar with each student. Smaller classes create more time for the professor to communicate with students about their assignments, grades, and performance. It is also easy to familiarize yourself with the library, classes, cafeteria and the overall campus. Most community colleges have honor societies such as Phi Theta Kappa and Alpha Gamma Sigma. Also, general classes such as English Composition, Fine Arts, Biology and more are offered at community colleges for cheaper rates than a university. In addition to cheaper courses, the room and board fees are cheaper as well. Why pay more money to the university for the same classes that can be taken at the community college?

For some students, one of the greatest reasons to attend community college is being granted financial aid without needing any student loans (your parent's income determines this factor). If you're lucky, you will earn a two-year degree without future debt. Yes! Attending community college is not a bad idea after all. You are winning at an early start.

Let's analyze the university, everything at universities are bigger from the campus to student population to the class size. They will possibly have more choices in clubs and organizations. Universities have sororities and fraternities that community colleges do not offer. A university offers a bachelor and master's degree. They also offer more classes relating to your chosen major. Of course, universities are more expensive but let's not forget there are more options and opportunities.

So, is it a good idea to attend a university? Yes, however it is not recommended until after you've had experience with a community college first or you have been granted a full academic scholarship or an athletic scholarship to the university. Keep in mind, if you desire a bachelor's degree, you have the option to take your first two years at a community college and then transfer to a university for the remaining two years. To assure things go smoothly with transferring, speak with a college counselor (before registering for classes). Now, that you have pondered a bit, what did you decide? Will it be a community college or university?

Note: To get a better idea, here is a quick breakdown of each: Starting with community college which has cheaper tuition, lower room and board fees, general courses (English Comp, Fine Arts etc.) are offered at community college for a lower cost. The student to faculty ratio at community colleges is lower than most four-year universities. The student population is smaller at community colleges. You may also obtain an associate's degree and have better interaction with the professor at the community college. Now, for the university, expenses are higher, larger student to faculty ratio, bigger student population, more opportunities, more clubs/organizations, Bachelor's and Master's degree are offered at the university.

Note: You can do a little more research, adding to the list and form the best decision for you.

WHICH DEGREE
LEVEL FITS YOU?

What level of degree are you seeking? Associates—Bachelors—Masters or Doctorate.

Knowing the level of degree to pursue, gives clear direction on which college to choose. Let's look at the different level of degrees. First, there is the associate's degree which is an undergraduate degree that can be obtained in two years. It requires a minimum of sixty semester hours or more and there are two options to choose from. The associate of arts degree which is designed to transfer course credits to a four-year university and the associate of applied science degree that differs by focusing on career courses for entry-level jobs, select courses can be transferred to a university as well.

The associate's degree can be completed at community colleges. A few career examples of an associate degree are avionics technician, radiation therapy and a computer specialist. If that's not quite what you are aiming towards, the bachelor's degree is the next level.

A bachelor's can be completed in four years at a university or in some cases, two years can be completed at a community college and the remaining can be completed at a university. This degree requires more time by requiring 120 semester hours or more. You will receive a higher salary with a bachelor's degree. There are also more alternatives within the job industry, after receiving this degree.

The Bachelor's (in most cases) does not restrict job seekers to one category of job fields. For example, if you received a degree in speech pathology, you could possibly apply for a position as a manager. Many employers only require a bachelor's degree to apply for the job. Career examples for the bachelor's degree are computer engineering and communications/broadcasting journalism.

The third level will be the master's degree. Typically, it can be earned within one to three years in addition to the bachelor's degree (depends on college and chosen major). The master's degree specializes in one field of study.

The last and highest level of degree is the Doctorate; this is an amazing accomplishment. The length of completing this degree depends on the field of study and the college you choose to attend. In many cases, the earning potential is greater as you seek the next degree level. Knowing the overview of each degree level can assist you in choosing which best fits your goals.

Checklist questions: What level of degree are you seeking? What is your plan for achieving this degree?

WHAT DOES THE COLLEGE OFFER?

Students often ask what does the college offer but the better question is what do you need the college to offer? What would make it a great fit for you? There is a series of questions to think about such as does the college offer your chosen major? The college catalog or website will provide that information. Don't forget about the days and times you wish to attend? Would you prefer day or night classes? Also, many colleges offer the same program of study however they may have different classes. For example, psychology at North College, may offer more general classes than those relating to psychology. South college may offer more classes pertaining to psychology than general courses.

Compare both college courses to one another, referencing your major. The classes that will be of value are those relating to your major. Now, what else does the college offer? If you've thought about online courses, confirm that the college offers this option and if so, are your classes available.

You can never be too choosy when it concerns your

education. Let's not forget, this is where you will spend lots of time and money. Speaking of money, is the tuition within your budget? How about the accreditation of the college? Is it or isn't it accredited? Course credits cannot transfer from an unaccredited college to an accredited college. So, it's important to research the college validation.

Next, many colleges allow students to stay the weekend on campus, while other colleges may not allow this choice. What does your college offer? Do they offer free tutoring? One more thought to bring into the light, are there any sororities, organizations or clubs that are important to you? What activities do you have in mind?

Checklist: What's on your list of things needed for the potential college?

LOCATION MATTERS

When I first started college, I chose a school two hours away from my hometown. I was so excited and ready to explore new places, activities, and eager to meet new friends. Upon my arrival to this new town I found it to be very small, so small in fact, the community of people who lived there knew one another by name. Activities and entertainment such as bowling, the movies or even a mall was non-existent. To experience that type of entertainment, students drove an hour to the next town. My finances wouldn't allow me to travel that far, so I settled for what I had, which was cable television in the dorm room. Aside from that, the college was decent with great instructors and a nice facility. I was truly grateful for the cafeteria food because there was only one drive-through restaurant in the surrounding area. Obviously, I did not do thorough research before picking the college.

The location of your college matters, think about the surroundings of the college and your satisfaction with it. Visit the campus and the city prior to finalizing your college choice. It really helps to be familiar with the surrounding area. Make a list of things you need to have a satisfying college experience. The location of the college is also important in terms of tuition fees. Many students travel across state to college, while the same education can be attained in-state or very close. The advantage of attending an in-state college is cheaper tuition. Plus, you don't have to travel far to visit family or vice versa.

Occasionally, there may be situations when you can't avoid going out of state because your in-state college does not offer the program of study. Living arrangements is another important aspect when deciding on college location. Like, are you staying on campus? If so, how far is the college from your home? Is the college walking distance of any shopping stores? Do you have transportation? Some of these questions should be thought about if deciding to commute as well.

Commuting is when students travel back and forth to college. Ask yourself questions such as how far will you be traveling? Will your finances allow you to make these trips? Even though commuting is the best way to save money for college expenses, be sure the college location is not far from home to allow this option. When deciding on location, don't base it on where your high school friend or boy/girlfriend attends. After socializing with others on campus, you may become distant with one another. Create more friends and meet new people.

Checklist question: What do you need in the surrounding area of the college? How far will you commute from home? Will your finances allow you to commute?

REASONS FOR ATTENDING COLLEGE

- *It's free to select students (depends on parent's income).*
- *College keeps you busy (in a positive way).*
- *Improve Communication Skills.*
- *Meet a diverse group of people.*
- *Join clubs and organizations.*
- *Learn a foreign language.*
- *Learning and Growing.*
- *Make solid friendships.*
- *Networking.*
- *Party.*

PART 5

PREPARING TO MEET YOUR ROOM MATE

INSIDE THE DORM ROOM

I was introduced to my first dorm room at Itawamba Community College. I occupied the attic style layout on the top floor. The room was made for three students however there were only two of us in the room. Walking into the room and to the right were twin size bunk beds and two desks. There was also a closet behind the door. To the left were a restroom and another bed which was sectioned off from the twin beds. I thought the room was spacious and unique. You can rearrange the room furniture, unless the college has strict rules against it.

The layout of dorms will be different at each college. The most common are residence halls which has a room that holds two people, the room space is typically small, beds are twin size and there is enough space for one small refrigerator (shared between you and your roommate), you may even share a T.V. The restroom is shared with several other ladies on the same floor as you; unless there is a private one in the room. Apartment style dorms have four rooms that occupy one person to each room; it includes the living room/kitchen space. To get a better vision of what dorm rooms look like, visit www.collegenewbies.com.

Note: Here are a few things you may experience, loud talking in the hallways, loud music when you're trying to sleep or study. Things will happen that will be beyond your control. Try not to panic or allow these things to get to you. After all, its college and many of your peers are running wild because there is no curfew or hovering parents.

UNDERSTANDING

Students, the mindset you have before arriving on campus will either help or hurt you. Remove all negative thoughts and horror stories pertaining to college that others have shared with you. Let's start fresh by first, preparing to understand others. Before meeting your dorm mate, it is important to know they will have different personalities, beliefs and background up-bringing. Your roommate could display some of the following behaviors such as quiet, out-spoken, good, weird, obnoxious or controlling among other things. The idea is not to be surprised by any actions that are unusual to you but accept them as a different individual.

Your dorm mate may not have been raised with the responsibilities such as being taught to clean behind themselves, doing laundry or even morals of being respectful. They may talk, act or even dress differently than you. People are different in many ways. These are things to keep in mind but hopefully you will get the best roommate anyone could wish for. Prior to their arrival, they may wonder, what type of person you are as well. You too, will have traits that may or may not be acceptable to others. If you understand this before your arrival to your room, you should have a good semester. Maintain a mature way of thinking about your roommate, not judgmental and things should go smoothly.

ARE YOU STUCK WITH A
DIFFICULT ROOMMATE?

No one is ever quite sure of what type of roommate they will be paired with. Students can only hope for the best. You and your roommate will be in each other's space most the time, so a pleasant atmosphere is needed. If we knew you would get an easy going and respectful roommate, these pointers wouldn't be necessary. However, that's not always the case, if you're unlucky and get paired with a difficult person. Here are a few pointers to keep the peace:

Calmly address issues immediately with your roommate if they occur. The last thing you want is an uncomfortable environment with such a long semester ahead. Not facing the issue could result in the situation getting worse. By chance, it becomes impossible to communicate with your dorm mate, inform someone in authority, and explain to them how you are being treated in the dorm room. You're probably thinking this will make things worse. In a case that you feel it will get worse, get advice from parents or friends who have been through similar situations.

It may be possible to change rooms or even get an empty room, granted, one is available. If the issue escalates, contact someone in the housing office. If you are afraid to speak up for yourself, it will be difficult to enjoy the remaining semester which could affect your studies. You deserve to be treated with respect in your room. Keep in mind you can always change rooms the following semester. Always avoid altercations to prevent fights.

COMMUNICATION

Communication is important in all relationships whether it's a professor, friend or whomever. It will be the bridge between you and your dorm mate as well as your peers during college. Communication builds relationships if expressed correctly. However, miscommunication or no communication can hurt relationships.

There will be times when you may need to talk with your roommate about things that bother you. To be successful during this conversation, there are three things you could do. *First*, be clear and direct about what you are saying. Do not play the role of being their parents because your roommate will get defensive in return. The *second* thing in communication is to refrain from expressing yourself jokingly or in a goofy way, if you do that, you will not be taken seriously. Am I saying act uptight? No, certainly not. Just be straight forward. The *third* thing is to have this conversation between you and your roommate. Do not have conversations in front of your friends because it will seem as if you are ganging up on him or her. Nor do you talk with them in front of their friends. It should only involve you and your roommate.

Always express issues that bother you, otherwise, no one will know how you feel. (Example) If your roommate eats your food without asking, that may be a problem for you. Calmly address the situation in a nice way.

How to express this to your dorm mate? You could say that you are on a budget and you don't have any extra food to share. This lets them know it is not okay and they should not do it again. You and your roommate will not always agree on things and that's totally understandable but holding issues to yourself, will make you angry or depressed about the environment you're in. Communicate with them as you would want them to communicate with you about anything that affects you.

To maintain your happiness and sanity, express yourself and most of the time, your dorm mate will listen to you. You could also ask your roommate if there is anything that you are doing that disturbs them as well? This will lighten the situation and show them that you are thoughtful. It is better to talk with them first before taking issues to an RA (Residents assistant) or another person of authority.

Note: Agreeing to dorm rules in the beginning would be a good idea.

EXPECTATIONS

To avoid disappointment and problems, do not expect anything from your roommate such as friendship. They could already have friends and choose not to make any new ones or you two may not have anything in common. Your dorm mate could be a loner, by choice. There could be many reasons they don't take interest in friendships but do not take it personal. However, engage in small talk with him or her. It is okay if you two are not friends but conversing will make things easier. If by chance, you two become best pals that would be awesome. Also, don't expect your roommate to share clothes, shoes or any other personal items.

PART 6

CLASSES

INSTRUCTOR

A professor's attitude towards you may depend on your demeanor in their classroom. Let's assume, you are the student whose grades are high, you're prompt for every lecture and you're always participating. It's likely the professor will take notice and enjoy having you as a student. However, doing the opposite such as being tardy or sleeping in class will make your professor frustrated. He will bring these things to your attention if you ever need extra credit.

Instructors are valuable to your academic studies and your future. The first mission upon entering class is to make yourself well-known to each of your instructors in a positive way. This does not mean become the professor's pet or pest. It simply means make connections with them.

Why should you do this? In the future, it's possible to request a letter of recommendation from professors or look to them as references for jobs. They may even assist you in finding a job.

How to make yourself known to the instructor?

You should introduce yourself on the first day at the

end of class, inform them of your major and say that you are looking forward to taking their class this semester. Make appointments to meet during their office hours. If you need assistance with assignments, contact them during office hours. Complete and submit all assignments on time, attend class, be on time, sit in the professors' sight and be respectful. You want them to remember good things about you. Once you connect with the professor and they've remembered you. You may feel more comfortable talking with them.

The second thing to remember about instructors is each instructor will teach differently, some teaching styles will be enjoyable and some will not, they will not necessarily entertain and do fun things in class. The main objective is to attend classes every day, absorb the information given, complete the class work, and submit homework to pass the class.

The professors are not responsible for incomplete assignments. They will not search for each student individually to inform them of missing assignments. If they do, consider yourself lucky. You may also attend a college with a large number of students, leading the professor not to take roll. It is still essential that you attend class (including rainy days). Go to class, even if your friend or classmate is willing to take notes for you. Why? Their notes may not be as effective or informative as yours would be. Don't trust anyone's information but your own.

PARTICIPATION IN CLASS

When you're in class, always participate in discussions, by doing so, you gain better understanding of the material. There is a great chance of understanding the material if you are discussing the information and an even greater chance of learning the information if you are practicing or explaining to others what you have learned.

When class ends, discuss with your roommate or a friend about the class topic to retain information. Repeat this cycle to increase chances of learning.

Participating in class includes responding to professors when they ask questions. There will be times when you don't have an answer in class but you may have a guess, don't be afraid to speak out. If you answer incorrectly, it happens to the best of us, try not to get discouraged. If you don't understand the lessons being taught, ask the professor to elaborate on the subject or write down the unclear statement and visit her or his office later to get an understanding.

GETTING COMFORTABLE IN THE CLASSROOM

Have you ever been uneasy when participating in groups, presenting presentations or answering questions?

Well, if your answer was yes, that feeling is common among students. In college, you will learn to face these types of challenges. If you are to reach your goals, you must develop skills to help you participate effectively. It may take time but gradually following these steps may put you at ease. The *first step* is sitting in the front row or very close to the front. Now, you're probably thinking "that's insane." Let me explain three reasons for seating yourself in the front.

The first reason is to give the professor your undivided attention. Focus completely and directly on the professor and the subject being taught. In doing this, you're able to block out your classmates because your attention is set on the professor. The second reason to sit in the front row is that the mind does not wonder as much while sitting in front of the classroom. You're practically forced to pay attention. Lastly, you're able to respond to professors in a normal tone versus yelling across the room.

Just imagine, if you sit towards the front and the professor called your name to answer a question, you could make eye contact with only her or him to respond. If by chance, you answer incorrectly, you may not feel embarrassed because students are unable to stare in your face if you're sitting up front. You are unable to see their faces as well which takes away the paranoid feeling of someone whispering or laughing at you. Now, imagine sitting in the back of the room and the teacher points to ask you a question. Some students will look in your face awaiting your reply, along with the instructor and this will immediately make you nervous. Your voice may start to tremble as you begin to speak. Now, which one seems more comfortable, sitting up front or in the back?

The *second step* to getting comfortable in the classroom is being comfortable in the classroom setting. How to make this setting more comfortable? Talk to students sitting next to you, become familiar with them (before or after class). Make appointments with the instructor, get to know him or her. Your objective is to talk with both the students and the instructor to lighten up the space and be comfortable in the classroom. The *third step* is being knowledgeable about the topics in class. Learning about the class material will allow you to become confident in your answers.

ONLINE CLASSES

Many students enroll in online courses full-time. This option is great for students with families and jobs. Online classes are great if you are self-disciplined, focused, and aggressive toward completing assignments on your own. An online class does not allow close interaction with professors. Communication is mostly through email, it will be possible to call the instructor but there will be set times he or she is available. All information needed for the class will be located on the syllabus or outline.

If you live near the campus, there is a chance you could make an appointment to visit the professor for tutor sessions or make-up work. The professor may require you to take final exams on campus. Aside from that, everything else is completed online. Online classes are accessible 24 hours; however, professors determine when you're allowed to begin assignments. They also determine the deadline for submitting the assignments. Online programs work around your busy schedules. If you don't have transportation or you're a busy parent or someone with a narrow schedule, online classes may work for you.

DIFFICULT COURSES

Growing up, I couldn't comprehend the lessons being taught in high school. I was so disappointed in myself, I felt like a failure academically. I thought to myself that I must be the slowest kid in class (I wasn't) but that's how I felt. Every day, from class to class I dreaded it because I wasn't as smart as other students. Most of my classmates didn't even take notes but could make straight A's. How is that possible? Some students missed classes a lot, came back and never missed a beat. They still made straight A's.

I took notes and never missed a day of school. Still, I was unable to comprehend the assignments given to produce A's or even B's. I strived for them however the C's category is where I landed every time. So, between the teachers and myself, something was missing, a link was broken, the connection was just not there. Soon, I realized, students learn differently, the information was being perceived and processed differently by each student. Everyone has different learning styles; you must figure out which learning style works best for you. Once you're aware of that, everything else falls into place. Although, I had difficult times in high school, I graduated a (C) average student.

After high school, my intentions were to attend college, regardless of my grades and I did just that. I guess something unraveled mentally during college because there was improvement in grades. After taking classes in college, I found that my ability to understand assignments had increased. I wondered how it was possible. How was I able to perform well in college and not so well in high school? College gives you options to choose professors, classes and times which increase chances of succeeding.

Students, do you remember those difficult classes you've taken in high school?

In college, you don't have to go through the same dreadful experience. You can approach these courses differently. Determine the difficult courses, take the basics first which is the easiest level. For example, you would take basic math before diving straight into college algebra. It will take longer by starting with the beginning subjects but it will help you pass the classes. Now that you've completed the basics, move into more complex classes.

Ensure you are receiving a good understanding and processing the information being taught before moving to the next level. Gaining a better understanding of each course, step by step builds your knowledge. The same rules apply to all subjects as well. Yes, this is a longer process but you have time. Do not view it as another class that will hold you in college longer. View it as facing a problem that you've been dealing with for a long time and now you are ready to conquer it. From High School to College, it is possible to improve!

STUDY GROUP

Study groups are good for students that are willing to go the extra mile. There is a strong chance you will excel in most classes, if the group is serious about the target goal. Cannot find a study group to join? Put one together yourself. This will also help others view you as a leader.

Groups are formed to assist one another with class and homework assignments. They also brainstorm ways to understand lessons being taught in class. Compare notes with each other to ensure nothing is missed. If a student in the group misses class, someone else could ensure that he or she is filled in on what they've missed. Study groups allow chances to make new friends, while learning material. The group should not exceed five people. As a group, you could also share ideas of how each of you prepare for tests.

STUDYING

When studying, find a method that works best for you to improve on work assignments. It can range from silently reviewing lecture notes or reading them aloud. On one discussion topic, try silently reviewing the notes and take notice the next morning to see if you remember the information. On a different discussion topic, try reading the notes aloud and notice if you remember the information the next morning or not. Which of these two methods help you retain the information most? You could also audio record daily lectures (if the instructor allows it) to re-play outside of class, jot down things that are confusing and meet with the instructor for a better understanding.

Students should study at least two hours for each class. Study hours can be broken into shorter times. You could try one hour before class and the other after class or when you have free time. This would not apply to test days as cramming information before a test may not provide good results. Cramming could cause confusion. Studying too much at once could be an overload on the brain and risk chances of not remembering what you studied. In between studying, take breaks, deep breaths and drink plenty of water.

Tip: If you're studying on a laptop or desktop. Take breaks often to avoid eyestrain.

PART 7

SOCIALIZING ON
CAMPUS AND
MAKING FRIENDS

INTERACT WITH PEERS

I remember the feeling of butterflies attacking my stomach before arriving on campus. I was extremely nervous. There were so many thoughts going through my mind:

"What will my roommate be like?"

"Will I make any new friends?"

"Will my classes be difficult?

The list goes on…

After arriving on campus and getting settled into the dorm, I watched my family leave which was the hardest part. I sucked it up and placed focus on meeting other students before the startup of classes.

I walked around campus to get a view of everything and hoped to bump into friendly faces but I didn't. I was far away from home without anyone on campus to talk to. I was not thinking that other freshman felt totally lost as I did. In fact, it looked like everyone was already well acquainted with each other. They were laughing, talking and standing in groups. I was the shy type, so there was no way I was going over to introduce myself.

I went back to the dorm and continued organizing my room. My roommate had not made it to the dorm yet, she arrived later that night, so we didn't have a chance to talk. I felt completely deserted on my first day. Of course, I moved in over the weekend. I told myself it would get better, that I just need to get comfortable being there.

The next day, I met my roommate and to my surprise, she was a Sophomore. She would talk but seemed distant. She already had friends so we didn't link up to become pals but we were pleasant and respectful of each other's space. Now that I think about my approach upon arriving to the campus, I understand where I went wrong. I evaluated myself, there were friendly faces but in return I didn't show a friendly face. I went back to the room instead of sitting in the girl's dorm lounge like everyone else. I didn't contact my roommate before arriving on campus to make things less awkward before she arrived. Most importantly, I didn't attempt to talk to anyone.

Students, when you arrive on campus, unpack and organize your room but make time to get back out of the room to meet other students. Talk, smile, ask questions and be aware of your facial expressions and body language. The social interaction between two people can be quite comforting, especially being a new kid on campus. These are a few ideas to think about when you arrive on campus.

Note: It's not weird to start a conversation with other peers. Someone has to do it, right? May as well be you. Good luck!

HOW TO MAKE FRIENDS?

Sometimes making friends can be a challenge, however it can be done. When attempting to make new friends, always be honest with yourself and the person you are befriending.

Rule number one when meeting peers, be you. Pretending to be someone or something you're not is false character and you will attract the wrong crowd. Try being yourself to attract the crowd that fits your personality and style. When making friends, hang with people who will accept you for who you are. Some people will make you feel bad about yourself whether it's intentional or not. For example, they may try to change things you like about yourself, don't do it. If you're satisfied with your actions, things you say or how you dress, that's all that matters.

Rule number two when trying to make friends, talk. You must converse and become a social butterfly to make a connection with others. When first meeting another student, do not think of them as a stranger. Just view them as another individual with the same intentions as you. You both may have similar conversation topics pertaining to college so don't worry too much about what you should or should not say, however think before you speak. Thinking before you speak allows the thought to process in your mind so the statement will be clear and understood.

If you see a potential friend, they could be someone in your class or your dorm. Start a conversation, say something like "What is your major?" If they seem friendly, continue talking, volunteer your major and go from there. If you're really comfortable, you could ask someone, "Where are you from?" After they've replied, tell them if you've ever visited their city with family or if you wish to go someday. Let them know where you're from and talk about things that are interesting in your hometown. When you run out of things to say, smoothly end the conversation. Talking is how you get to know one another.

Before class begins, strike up a conversation with someone seated next to you. Start with simple things like hi. If that person doesn't seem interested in talking, cool. Try sitting next to a different person the following day, use the same technique.

The more you do this, the more confident you will get when approaching people. You may talk with these people only for that moment or you may link up to become friends. Don't get discouraged if friendships are not formed. Everyone is not compatible. Many students meet by getting involved in similar activities on campus; while others are more social and out-going.

Rule number three is to listen. This is very important when having a conversation with someone, it can get annoying when talking with someone and they're not paying attention to what you're saying as if it's not important. Show common courtesy and listen to the other person. Nod your head and make eye contact with a few words like really? That's interesting. People are always in need of someone to listen to their plans, problems or what they've done over the weekends. Overall, no one will be an outcast in college, unless he or she chooses to be. You will meet a variety of students on campus and fit in perfectly.

Note: Some students are not able to fully experience the social life they desire due to the demanding assignments, test, essays and possibly a job.

CHOOSE YOUR CROWD

The crowd you choose to hang around may decide the impact of your college experience. Choose people who are like-minded individuals. Interact with students who are serious about their education.

How will you know?

The *first pointer* is observation, if the person you want to befriend is in class with you; observe their behavior, if they are always late for class, he or she have excuses for missed assignments, has a pattern of missing classes when it rains or if this person sleeps while in class, then that may not be the person to hang around. It doesn't mean they are a bad person. Their priorities may not be in order and bad habits can be contagious if allowed into your space.

To my *next point*, listening to conversations is the second way to choose your crowd. When your potential friend is talking, listen to what they're talking about. General conversation like the weather, clothes, family, classes or goals is all good but if they are gossiping and speaking negative; you may not wish to engage with these students. Listen carefully to conversations and decide if you wish to be in their presence.

Actions are the third and final way to choose your crowd. Actions will let you know if they deserve your presence. Compulsive drinking, smoking, chasing girls or boys, disrespectful behavior or being rude to others may not be a good sign that this person should be in your chosen crowd.

To increase the chances of having a successful life in college, choose a crowd that will motivate you, choose people with positive attitudes and goals. Figure out their hobbies, find out the places they like to hang out. The point is to ensure you two have the same common goals. Goals are not the same for all students. Yes, you should experience new things and learn from others but those things should be positive, interesting or anything that you feel is right. Wrong crowds will steer you in the wrong direction.

Hanging with a negative crowd is a bad choice because they may not be interested in their studies. They may not work as hard finishing assignments and studying. Other students can be persuasive and it's even worse when you are bored.

Do not lie to yourself and think that you have control over your decisions. While that may be true, there are others who can distract you from that positive thinking. Is this what you want in your life? What decision will you make? What crowd will you share your presence with?

Note: It may seem like a lot to observe your peers; listen to conversations and notice their actions but I assure you. It doesn't take long to know if you want someone in your circle. These are just things to look for.

Note #2: I'm not saying be judgmental towards others. I am saying be selective with picking friends/acquaintances. Why? You will spend lots of time with these people.

BE AWARE OF YOUR SURROUNDINGS

When you go out with others always be aware of your surroundings. Safety may not be the first thing that comes to mind when you're headed out for fun. However, it is important to stay free of danger. Know where you're headed. Who you're with? And what type of vehicle you're getting into? This information can be given to someone you trust as a safety precaution.

If possible, try not to go anywhere alone; stay in groups or couples to avoid criminals or violent activities. If you go to a party and decide to drink, never sit the cup down or accept drinks from others. You should not trust anyone to hold it for you because someone could easily slip a drug or anything into the cup. Why would anyone do this? One reason would be to take advantage of you.

Avoid getting wasted on alcohol beverages. If your friends are drinking and driving, don't get into the car with them. Think about your future and those who love you, make wise decisions at all times. Do not think, "well, one time won't hurt anybody," just once could turn your life into a downwards spiral. Ask to drive or call another source for transportation. If something does not feel right, it's probably not. Also, everyone who smiles at you does not always have your best interest at heart. Have fun but be safe. This is not to scare you but only to make you aware of what's happening on some college campuses.

Note: Encourage your friends not to drink and drive.

HAVE FUN

College life should be a fun experience. Yes, you should take your work assignments and grades seriously. However, having fun is part of the experience. College is the time to be open to new ideas, finding your inner creativity and networking.

Many students refer to college fun as partying, drinking (getting wasted) and even smoking marijuana. That type of fun is not for everyone, although it does take place in college. College fun is whatever sparks your interest, not your friends, your roommates or other peers but you.

What are you interested in? You may seem like an odd ball if you don't engage in what the crowd is doing but don't lose focus or follow any crowd to fit in. There is so much you could do to make this experience great, do not limit yourself.

College will be your new home for a while so get comfortable in that setting. Try socializing. Your social life will matter, avoid isolating yourself in a room, even if you prefer to be alone, make at least one friend or acquaintance for company. If you are the shy type, find a way to meet people. If you are the out-going type, mixing with the crowd should not be a problem for you.

The key to it all is to be active. Active students are self-motivated with upbeat spirits. Search different clubs and activities on your campus and join. For example, there are sororities if you like to show off your dancing skills, the band for anyone who loves music, for sport lovers, basketball, baseball, or football may interest you. It doesn't matter which organization you join or which sport you play. Enjoy the moments to create good college memories.

If you decide not to join any clubs or play sports, that is acceptable. You could do other things like hit the workout room to stay healthy or go to the library and read a book. You could form a book club or join a church choir near the school if you like to sing. Ladies, you could invite people from your hall or close friends to host a movie night with snacks to eat. Ensure that your dorm mate is included or check to see if it's good with her prior to doing this. Guys, you could have a video game challenge with friends. Check with your dorm mate as well.

Fun is great while we want to be respectful to your roommate's space. Don't forget to take plenty of pictures. You will want to capture those happy memories. Having fun is helpful during those stressful moments in college.

8 TIPS TO IMPROVE SOCIAL SKILLS ON CAMPUS

1. Listen entirely to what the other person is saying.

- Do not interrupt them while they are talking.
- Be sure to understand what they have said, if you are not sure, ask for clarification.

2. Respond to what they have said by making a comment or asking a question.

- Think before you make a comment.
- Ask questions without making it sound like an interrogation.

3. Do not change the subject until the other person finishes the conversation.

- Give feedback about their conversation.

4. Make simple suggestions or say "May I offer you a bit of advice.

- Sometimes people just need to vent.

5. If the person you are conversing with is talking about something that effects or affected them. Do not overtake the conversation by turning their problem into a similar issue or situation you've had.

- You're allowed to relate but don't take the focus from their conversation.
- You can tell them about your similar situation only after their done expressing themselves.

6. Stay present in the conversation.

- Try not to wonder in your own thoughts.
- Keep your responses relevant to the conversation.

7. Open-up to different conversations.

- Even if you are not interested in what is being said continue talking because what you want to discuss may not be interesting to them either.

8. Know when to end the conversation.

- Try not to end the conversation abruptly.
- Be smooth and inform them in a nice way.

PART 8

WHAT IS YOUR
CHARACTER?

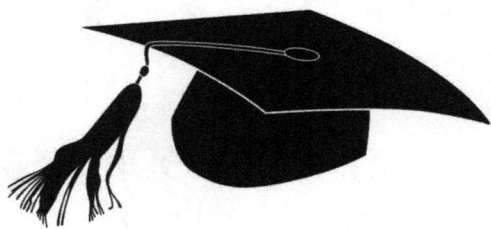

LEADERSHIP

Are you a natural born leader or does your skills need developing? If you don't already possess these skills, don't fret, it can be obtained through practice. Leadership is the ability to guide, direct, or influence people. This characteristic is important in life, when others follow your lead, you may be more focused and motivated to do greater things.

Why?

People are counting on you. They may have admiration for the high goals you set for yourself and the positive role you play in others' lives. A leadership role comes with great responsibility, clear communication, and someone who is not afraid to express their opinions and make decisions. Being a leader takes courage.

College is a great starting point in developing leadership skills. In college, being a leader will be helpful in group activities, class participation or presentations. Professors may volunteer you for specific projects, if they feel you could be a leader. This is also an advantage for life after college. Many employers search for people who have leadership abilities (in many cases). Those who have these abilities increase chances to receive higher positions.

Your siblings may even be inspired by your will to take charge of situations, so always be a positive leader in life. You never know who will be watching. Leadership skills build your self-esteem and increase possibilities. Remember, be the leading type, not the bossy type. There is a difference.

Question: Have you ever acted as a leader at church, high school or a family gathering? Have you ever wanted to be a leader? College can help you fulfill that role.

WHO ARE YOU?

How well do you know yourself? This question is extremely important. Learning about who you are will take time, it can't be summed up overnight and that's okay.

Now that you're in college, others opinions and beliefs will be shared amongst each other, there is a possibility that your views, opinions, hobbies and activities will change. Sometimes that can be great as it allows you a chance to evolve or think outside the box. On the flip side, absorbing a negative mindset or participating in dangerous activities with peers will become unpleasant.

You must be able to think and make decisions on your own, otherwise, you may live a life that is not your own. Do not allow the persuasion of others interfere with your thinking. If you don't know who you are, you leave yourself open to anyone's habits or ideas. Other students' decisions become yours, other's thinking become yours. Learn to stick with the choices you make because you must live with any consequences behind them. Understand how to use helpful information and throw away the rest.

During this college experience, you will learn a lot about yourself. Write down simple questions to answer:

- What do you like to do for fun?
- What makes you happy?
- Where do you see yourself in five years?

Any details you could learn about yourself would be great. Always be honest with yourself. As time passes you will learn new and interesting things. When you understand who you are, you can make solid and confident decisions on your own. Just remember not to allow anyone else to answer these questions for you. You should answer from within your own mind and heart. Be firm with what you say and how you act, everyone will not accept it but at least you are aware of who you are.

Note: Learning about yourself can be a fun journey; it doesn't have to be an unpleasant experience.

IT'S OKAY TO SAY NO

Are you the "yes" person? Are you the person that wants to make everyone happy? There is nothing wrong with that attitude until you say yes when you really want to say no. There is nothing wrong with making others happy if it doesn't make you unhappy in the process.

For example, if a friend asks you to drink alcohol because they didn't want to drink alone. You're allowed to say no. This will not make you any less cool. P.S. Real friends won't pressure you into anything you dislike.

What are two things that you normally say "yes" to but you really want to say no?

_____

_____

After mentally deciding to say no, write two ways you will respond in the future.

_____

_____

IT'S OKAY TO SAY YES

Are you the "no thanks" type of individual? Well, there is nothing wrong with that personality either, however sometimes opening up to others builds relationships. For example, if a peer invited you to an activity on campus, instead of turning down the invitation. Perhaps, you could carve time into your schedule and head out. You may just enjoy yourself.

Name 4 reasons you say "no" to social events, academic clubs, invitations or activities.

_____

_____

_____

_____

RESPONSIBILITY

You are responsible for everything that needs to be done while you're in college such as shopping for personal items, studying for test, finishing class work or homework, getting to class everyday (even on rainy days) you are responsible for doing laundry, cleaning your room and all that other good stuff.

Responsibility sounds like a scary word, right? Don't let that scare you, it just means that you are taking charge of your life, is that what you want? You want to go out on the town and party. You want space from your extra-loving parents that won't let go. You want to make your own decisions. That is all great but only after prioritizing your college duties.

In order to prioritize in a smooth manner, a calendar will be needed. Note everything that may be of importance to you. Yes, your syllabus will have test dates but also write important dates on your calendar. The calendar should be placed in your vision for a reminder of your daily task.

Get creative with your college tasks and deadlines. For example, if time permits, laundry can be done through the week to avoid being swamped on the weekends. This will give you extra time to do other things. After you finish laundry, mark the next day to iron your clothes for the following week; these chores allow you to sleep a little longer and not rush to class. Everything will be organized in advance. Studying should be penciled in often, this way anxiety will not creep in on test day, at least not as much.

If things get stressful for you, relax and take time to unwind and give your mind and body rest. When peers are pressuring you about hanging out but you should be studying, ask yourself. "What is more important, going to the mall or studying for an upcoming test?" We often put the important things aside to have fun and later make excuses. However, responsible students place academics over a good time.

DRESS CODE

Are you worried about dressing the part? The new kid on the block tends to wonder, "How should I dress?" If I were you, I wouldn't lose sleep over it. No one cares if you're the best dressed person in school. There are no dress codes for college. Am I saying you're granted to step on campus looking abandoned? No. I'm saying you have the freedom to wear whatever you like. The great part is, the below advice provides tips to look nice, while saving money. Jeans, tee-shirt and nice shoes will be the normal. Let's talk about the hair, clothes, and shoes.

HAIR:

Ladies, we tend to stress about hair and the way it looks. If at some point, striving for the perfect curls get tiresome. A cute pony-tail will do the trick. Braids will also hold you over through the week and possibly the month, depending on the style. Try manageable hair styles you could do yourself. Any style you choose, ensure it doesn't break the bank. There is no need to spend lots of money at salons every week; this money can go toward food or other dorm items.

Guys, it is okay if you decide skipping a week without a haircut. Unlike high school, you can wear hats in college and no one will criticize you for it. They won't even tell you how to wear it. Sounds good?

CLOTHES:

Everyone has their own style in clothing. Some people like the simple look, as I mentioned before jeans and a t-shirt. That's original and it never gets old. A vast number of students, male and female will dress this way. Ladies may wear a nice blouse with their jeans to make it cute and the guys may wear a button down or polo to make their style pop.

Another look people could gravitate to is wearing the University name. Example: Ole Miss University or the University of Memphis—T-shirt, long sleeves and even sweats are sold with the college name on them. It's cool to represent the college you attend. These clothes can be found in the college store or even online. Students alternate from college name clothes to regular clothing but that's a style to adopt.

Don't feel pressured to buy new clothes and shoes. Trust me, not everyone will follow that route. Once you get on campus and get a feel of things, you will see that it's not all that you expected. You will see different "looks" all over campus. Whatever makes you feel comfortable, you should go for it.

Here is a side note: If you joined a sorority, they may expect more from you. You will possibly be pressured to dress the part, belonging to such a respectable group. There is a strong chance they want your standards to be higher; they'll want your appearance to be nothing less than spotless because you will no longer represent an individual (you) but a group.

SHOES:

Shoes are inexpensive for both males and females. Even when you are sporting inexpensive shoes, you can feel fashionable and look great. For starters, young ladies can wear cute sandals, wedges or boat shoes. Ladies have worn heels on campus, this is ok however be mindful that classes are across the street and around the block and it will take longer for you to get to class, plus your feet may get sore walking long distances in high heels every day. Wear shoes that are comfortable.

Guys can opt for sneakers, sandals and boat shoes as well. There is a trick to looking nice without going broke on campus. These tips are a great way to do that.

Clothes should always be clean and neat. It helps your character with peers and professors. There is a great chance, you'll see peers in pajamas but don't follow that trend. Remember, you want to make connections with the instructor in a positive way.

The way professors view you is very important. Try to look presentable. Dressing nice will boost your confidence. In college, no one is in competition with your wardrobe. College is nothing like high school where everyone made fashion a big deal. Students are too busy with classes, work and other things to be concerned about what you're wearing. Overall, keep a nice appearance and everything else will work perfect.

A WINNER'S CHARACTERISTIC PERSEVERANCE

If this book doesn't move you to do anything else, allow it to create a sense of perseverance within you. Perseverance is the quality that allows someone to continue doing something or trying to do something even though it is difficult. That single word "perseverance" is how I received my college degree.

Perseverance is going when no one else is around to push you. It's when you feel you have everything to lose and you can't give up. It is a desire you create inside yourself, so when you get tired and want to quit. It keeps going. You will not fail being a student of perseverance. In a competitive environment, perseverance is an invaluable asset.

Now, what's so important about perseverance? Well, it leads you to a piece of paper called a college degree. That piece of paper is a reminder to yourself that you can be dedicated and finish what you start. This magical piece of paper gives you the option to compete in today's workforce. The message that I want to carve into each of your minds is to be persistent in receiving your degree.

It's easy for students to give up and drop out. Some have given up on college because everything was handed to them. They were given the golden platter at a young age by their parents. Many others quit because it was a pattern they saw very often growing up. Their family and friends never finished projects. So, they didn't feel pressured to finish what they started. You have been programmed to follow the footsteps of your parents or those who raised you, good or bad that's usually how it works. Today, you can break the cycle of acting on what you've seen in your childhood.

Put aside that golden platter and create your own destiny with your sweat and hard work. You can now say that you will be the strong-minded person in your family to break the cycle of giving up. So, again I say perseverance is a very important tool for college and throughout your life.

REASONS FOR
ATTENDING COLLEGE

- *Overcome Shyness- forced to do individual speeches.*
- *Take advantage of student activities on campus.*
- *You may find college easier than high school.*
- *Train yourself to be prompt for future jobs.*
- *Learn to observe and analyze situations.*
- *Become responsible and independent.*
- *Learn to manage your money.*
- *Learn critical thinking skills.*
- *Learn to meet deadlines.*
- *Learn to do laundry.*
- *Challenge yourself.*

PART 9

PERSONAL SAFETY & SECUREMENT

SEXUAL ASSAULT

Sexual assault is a form of sexual violence, any involuntary sexual act in which a person is threatened, coerced, or forced to engage against their will, or any non-consensual sexual touching of a person. As stated before, this type of assault is increasing among college campuses in various states. All students should be aware of this act before arriving on campus. Many assaults that have taken place are usually by someone the victim knows. Here are a few things to do to avoid this situation.

One, ladies do not hang with a group of guys in private, being the only female. Two, do not overindulge with alcohol in the presence of people you don't know. This is the easiest way for someone to take advantage of you. Many young women are being sexually assaulted on college campuses and sometimes they are not aware until it's over. Three, do not go to a guys' dorm room. If you wish to see a male friend, invite him to your room while your roommate is there or leave the door open. You two could meet in the student's lounge or somewhere on campus in public. Lastly, always carry pepper spray with you.

Sexual assault happens to guys as well but it's not commonly reported for fear of what others will say and think. Guys, the most important way to avoid sexual assault is to never get drunk (wasted) around anyone. Also, pay attention to other guys' conversations and actions. If they make you feel uneasy, avoid hanging out with them. Guys, never be afraid to speak out in a case like this. You have every right to voice an issue like this. Sexual assault is not to be taken lightly.

On the other hand, don't be the person to commit these acts. Refuse to be persuaded to engage in disturbing behaviors. Think clearly about the situation, there is only one place guilty parties could go after this incident. Jail, meaning your freedom is no longer yours. After being released from jail, you will have a record that is attached to your name (forever). Employers will not hire you. Others will continuously judge you, regardless of how good you may be doing at that present time. Having family of your own, would you want someone to do this to them? Think about the children you may have in the future; would you want them to learn you engaged in such activity. An incident like this could haunt you for years to come. Both male and female should report any incidents and seek counseling to express what you're feeling. This is a serious matter and all assaults should be reported immediately.

Note: An assault does not only happen among the opposite sex, this could happen from those of the same sex as well. If you are aware of anyone sexually assaulting students, tell someone.

MEDICAL CONDITIONS IN CLASSROOM AND DORM ROOMS

Students if you have any medical conditions such as epileptic seizures, narcolepsy or even asthma attacks. It would be a good idea to share it with your roommate and professor. An epileptic seizure is a brief episode of signs and/or symptoms due to abnormal excessive activity in the brain. A seizure temporarily interferes with muscle control, movement and speech. This condition causes a person to shake uncontrollably for a few seconds to a few minutes. Narcolepsy is another medical condition, they experience periods of extreme daytime sleepiness and cannot control it, leading them to fall asleep any time. You may fall asleep in the classroom. Therefore it's important to inform your professor on the condition. You wouldn't want them to think you're being rude or disrespectful.

There are also medical conditions such as asthma attacks, a sudden worsening of asthma symptoms caused by the tightening of muscles around your airways. If your roommate knows about your medical condition, they can assist you when they occur. They could really panic, if you were to have one of those moments, and they're unsure of what to do. This is not to bring attention to you but for their knowledge. They will be aware and know the steps he or she needs to take. If you have specific directions for them to follow, let them know.

DISABILITIES IN COLLEGE

Check the college handbook to view options for students with a disability. If the handbook doesn't provide enough information, call the college well in advance. Dyslexia is an example of a disability. Dyslexia a learning disorder characterized by difficulty reading due to problems identifying speech sounds and learning how they relate to letters and words.

PERSONAL ITEMS

Janice, a freshman in college was very trusting of her roommate, even though they weren't the best of friends. Like many other students, she'd been warned of all the horror stories about college roommates but her roommate appeared to be a trusting person, it never crossed her mind that the roommate was a thief.

One day Janice was in a rush and left her purse, which contained her social security card. As time passed Janice learned her social security number had been stolen, if you guessed by the roommate, you guessed correct. Not only did she steal her social security card but her credit was ruined and her identity was no longer hers alone, the roommate had stolen that too. Learning of the theft was only the beginning. It will be a long and hard road trying to straighten out such a misfortune as this.

Students, bring a lock box to place all important papers. Do not leave social security cards lying around. Someone could steal your identity with that information. If you do not need it (social security card) for a job or any other reason, it's best to leave that along with other personal items home. Do not trust that your roommate or your roommate's friends will not ramble through your things. Credit cards, check books, driver license and money should all be placed away in a safe place.

PART 10

THINGS THAT HELP AFTER COLLEGE

AFTER COLLEGE

Your journey does not stop after college graduation. This is the point when things get a little frustrating and busy. Why? It's time to apply for positions at numerous of places and wait for that magical call. It may be difficult to find employment immediately after graduation in your chosen career field. The good news is that you could also apply for positions in another career field. Many jobs only require an associates or bachelor's degree to apply for the job. This gives you options until you can proceed with your intended career but who knows, you may even become interested in your alternate outcome of employment. If it seems impossible to get hired, try working at local companies in the area but never stop applying for positions in your career field. Will you have a college degree to make that choice? I'm positive that you will, jobs requiring a degree pay more. The degree also provides more opportunities. Regardless of what happens after college, never give up and always strive to do your best.

Note: Find employment soon as possible (doesn't have to be in your field of study).

EXPERIENCE

Sometimes, when we choose a career that pays well, the outcome may not be what we've expected. For instance, a friend of mine attended the University of Memphis, graduated and received a degree in business management. She uploaded resumes online, applied with local companies. She did everything possible to find a satisfying job. Finally, she found employment at a healthcare facility caring for elderly patients but here is the problem, she was only earning $8.00 an hour.

Am I serious? Yes, very much so. Now, it sounds bad and really, it is bad. She worked her butt off for four to five years and taken out student loans only to get $8.00 an hour. Now, there are many ways to perceive this situation. I encouraged her to keep the job for experience because employers require 1-2 years of experience plus your degree. Some even require more experience than that. Since she was unemployed, what did she have to lose? My friend took my advice, kept the job. Later, she was promoted within the company and today she is a manager at that same healthcare facility earning a much greater income. Two years for the amount she's earning is a great trade. She is still young and opportunities are still out there if she decides to do something different. She now has the degree and the experience. If you're blessed or lucky, you will graduate, get a job that pays extremely well and not worry about any situations like these.

INTERNSHIP

Students, internships are essential to life after college. What is an internship? It's a program that provides practical experience for beginners in an occupation or profession. Some are paid while other internships are unpaid. It's possible to get an internship while you're attending college. Interning during college provides experience which can be put on your resume. Following graduation, you will be prepared to immediately apply for positions and you will also have a better idea of your career. Granted, the internship coincided with your chosen major.

Many students may intern after graduation. This is not a bad idea; any internship is an advantage due to the experience gained. Employers may take a chance on students with intern experience versus those who lack any experience.

HOW IMPORTANT IS NETWORKING?

Networking is the process or practice of building up or maintaining informal relationships, especially with people whose friendship could bring advantages such as a job or business opportunities. As a student, you're in a great position to start networking. Your goal is to converse with people to leave great lasting impressions.

How would you do this?

Attend student activities on campus, even the ones that may not interest you. For example, if you learned that a guest speaker will be visiting your college. Research the speaker past videos and projects to learn more about them. Find out their speech topic and gather relevant questions pertaining to that topic. On the day of the seminar, sit close to the front and ask questions (if they allow them), meet and greet with them personally to make a connection. Get their business cards, website address and ask additional questions about their speech or about their career. Try not to sound like you're interrogating but rather interested. You could volunteer your major and briefly inform her or him of your plans after graduation.

Another way to network on campus is conversing with professors on campus. You don't have to be enrolled into their class to make this happen. Let's not forget about the librarian, other students, campus security, and many other administrators that could be easily over-looked. Through the process of networking, keep a positive attitude and be persistent, well-mannered and respectful. Lastly, you shouldn't burn any bridges along the way. You never know who you may meet again in the future.

PART 11

THINGS THAT
HELP WHILE
IN COLLEGE

WAYS TO EARN EXTRA CASH WHILE IN COLLEGE

Times get tough on campus when you're lacking a steady financial income to buy food or necessary items. Here are a few ideas to assist you in earning cash while in college. Pick a subject you're great at and tutor other students for a small fee. Remember, they may not have funds either, so keep the price reasonable. You could also take used clothes and items to stores that buy/sell and/or pawn shops. Not only could you take your old goods, ask your parents and relatives for items they no longer use. After each semester, sell your books on Amazon or EBAY. First, ensure the book is not needed for an upcoming course.

Note: The College won't pay much for used books.

WORK STUDY

Applying for work-study should be a part of your career planning. It allows students to work part-time on campus while earning income to help with school expenses. Working and attending college will also look great on your resume. Working shows experience in the work field, this is needed because there are employers who will not hire you without experience, even after college. You're going to think, "well, how will I ever get a job if no one takes a chance on hiring me without work experience?"

Don't worry, it may be difficult in the beginning but eventually someone will hire you. Work-study shows the employers you are a motivated individual and not afraid of multiple tasks at once. Work-study is on campus (in most cases), which is convenient for students to have their appointed job, classes and dorm room in the same area. Working while in college, allows you to interact with other people, resulting in better communication skills.

One of the many important advantages of work-study, is requesting a letter of recommendation from leading administrators whom you've worked for (a good work ethic would help). If work-study is available for you, take advantage. Depending on your job and how well you perform it, you could possibly apply for a position at the college after graduation.

GIVE YOURSELF THE
GIFT OF DISCIPLINE

The best gift a college student can give themselves is discipline, there will be times when you want to hang out with friends, go to parties, attend a sporting event or play video games. There is nothing wrong with that, many tempting situations will occur during college. Staying on track with assignment deadlines, achieving high scores and class attendance should be a priority. This requires self-discipline in which you already possess for the most part, how do I know? Well, for starters, you had to get up every day for high school and be on time. Sure, you had a little help from mom being a human alarm clock but you can replace her with a digital clock (sorry mom). Approach college knowing what you wish to accomplish and embed an attitude of "I got this," "I can do this" and "I will not stop until I receive my degree." Students are more likely to succeed in college if they know why they're attending in the first place. Think about this, if you enroll in college only because your friend is attending, what would happen if that same friend decided to drop out the next semester?

Will you drop out as well? What would be your motivation for continuing? Students, make plans for your future, even if they're not crystal clear, you can always change them later. Be disciplined.

PART 12

THINGS THAT
SLOW YOU DOWN

DISTRACTIONS

You may have your share of distractions throughout college, whether it be a roommate, peers, sports, family or it could simply be your own thoughts. You may be completing assignments, at work, or studying and they just pop up. Distractions will arise and when they do, turn your attention back to the present moment. Be conscious of what you are doing at that moment. Distractions can easily consume you.

I was in a two-year relationship when I first began college. Yes, this was my distraction. It was very difficult for my boyfriend and me to maintain a healthy relationship. He was a professional truck driver while I was a student in college. We began having trust issues with one another due to the long distance. He was very skeptical about my loyalty to him as I was surrounded by many other young guys on campus. Yes, I was faithful, so faithful in fact that I was unable to have a pleasant social life. I didn't want to attend parties, afraid he would think I was talking to other guys, so I avoided it all together. I was also skeptical of his actions, which was frustrating. This made it difficult for me to concentrate on my studies.

No student, male or female should have experiences like this. As a college student, you should be able to experience activities without thinking, what will my boy/girlfriend think? If you two continue to date, you must have trust for it to work. If you two decide to have a long-distance relationship. You and your partner should have a mutual understanding, prior to college.

During your time in college, you will not be able to communicate as much as you like due to studying, assignments, and other things. If they are not understanding to your needs, maybe it's time for space between the two of you. Figure out what is more important to you, college degree or the relationship. I understand both are big deals however, someone with the same goals as you will not hinder your achievements. It's possible to have both, just prioritize.

Know what comes first and what comes later. Your distraction could be something very different from mine. You might become distracted with late night parties even though you have morning classes. This causes you to be absent from class. When that happens, try partying on weekends to attend weekday classes on time. You may even get distracted with a full-time job. Employers sometimes have mandatory overtime. This interferes with your studying and completing assignments. Your education is more important, try finding a part-time position to better align with your schedule. Remove all distractions to solely focus on furthering your education.

REASONS FOR ATTENDING COLLEGE

- *If you're good in sports, there is a chance to be recognized by a recruiter in college.*
- *If you work, use school credit when filing income tax to get more money back.*
- *You can choose the days and times you would like to attend classes.*
- *You may meet a nice young lady or young man to date.*
- *You can receive scholarships and grants.*
- *To experience living away from home.*
- *To keep your brain active and sharp.*
- *Discover things about yourself.*
- *To graduate for a second time.*
- *To build your confidence.*
- *To inspire your siblings.*

PART 13

WHEN TIMES
GET ROUGH

IN CASE YOU
BECOME STRESSED

Juggling different classes with many assignments, homework, test and essays can be stressful at times. Some students get stressed to a point of wanting to give up and go home. During times like these, it can be helpful to step away from the work overload to re-gain a clear mind. This is when you take time for yourself. That hobby that you love to do; now is the time to do it. If you don't have a hobby, try taking pictures of things with your phone or camera.

Things like what?

You can take pictures of art, nature or even other people. You could also make a video on a topic you have a lot of knowledge about. Meditation, yoga and exercise will calm you as well. This will occupy your mind from the problems (at least for a while). After clearing your mind of stressful issues, it may be easier to tackle deadlines and complete assignments.

PATIENCE IN COLLEGE RUSHING THROUGH COLLEGE

It's possible to become impatient and frustrated and lose the excitement of attending college. If this happens, you may start to rush through college. Meaning, you may take shortcuts and in result, settle to receive a career certificate instead of an associate's degree or you may be satisfied with an associate's degree in place of your aim to receive a Bachelor's degree.

When you become impatient, something else could be taking your attention away from your education such as a long-distance relationship which can be fixed with more visits to one another. Another reason for impatience to occur is the tiring cycle of going to class every day, writing long essays and becoming overwhelmed. This is the time to prioritize classes and work assignments. Decide which classes require your attention most. Which class has upcoming test? After deciding which is most important; begin working on assignments soon as possible. It doesn't have to be completed at once but starting the assignment will help or if you choose to study, do so immediately after class.

Patience is needed when attending college. Keep in mind the things you want for your future. This helps you focus and keeps you moving forward. There is always time to do extra things that interest you. Rushing through college will lower your scores as you will not be focused on your classes. Try not to look at the length of a major, manage each semester one at a time. If you begin college, put your best efforts forward to graduate.

14 REASONS TO FINISH COLLEGE

1. You can apply for jobs that many others cannot.
2. The higher the Education- the higher your salary (In most cases).
3. It looks good on your resume.
4. It shows you have goals in life.
5. To gain respect from others.
6. To be qualified for a specific job.
7. Make your family proud.
8. Feel happy about a huge accomplishment.
9. Silence those who said you wouldn't make it.
10. Investment that will return funds.
11. Many jobs require an Associates or Bachelor's degree.
12. To honor those who possibly could not attend college but wanted to.
13. To be the first in the family to graduate.
14. Build a strong foundation for your kid(s).

DO YOU HAVE AN URGE TO DROP OUT OF COLLEGE?

There are many students that drop-out of college. Some decide to enter the workforce full time. Others miss family, friends and their familiar surroundings and many just decide college isn't for them. These reasons are ok. However, before you decide against college. Think about a few things first such as:

"What will you do when you return home with family?"

"Are your home town friends doing something productive that motivates you?"

"Will that familiar surrounding help your career or advance you in any way?"

"Do you really want to owe a debt (student loans) without getting a college degree?"

If you start and you don't think college is for you, there are options such as changing your major to a one-year program. For example, the EMT- Basic program. It can be completed in a short period. These options depend on the college you're attending and the major chosen. Certain careers may not pay well but you could receive a career certificate.

Still don't think college is for you? Try taking online courses from home. This way, you could work and still receive a degree while going at your own pace. It is always an advantage to have graduated college. It looks great on a resume and job applications. After obtaining a degree, you will always have a back-up plan for employment.

YOU CAN DO THIS

Students! You are intelligent, regardless of your grades in high school. You are important, regardless of what others say and you have potential, regardless of your background. You can be whoever you imagine yourself to be. You can become whatever you decide to be. You must do a few things first. Work hard, stay focused, dedicate yourself to your future and never let other people tell you that you can't achieve something.

Do not limit yourself to certain jobs if you know you can achieve more. If you believe you can do something. Go for it and do not wait for someone else to give you a green light because sometimes it doesn't work that way. You cannot be unproductive with expectations of receiving that career you dream about. You must take your time and learn the steps to being a part of your dream.

Do not talk yourself out of your own success. Believe in yourself and never settle with comfort, unless that's where you want to be.

To become successful, put in time and effort and not

just verbally say what you want. Success is an "action" word and once you find the path that is right for you. Take it! Stay focused and Good Luck.

PART 14

ASIDE FROM COLLEGE

GROWING & LEARNING

Never be afraid to learn new things in college, on the job, at church or anywhere. Always be open to new opportunities. Watch a variety of movies and read a variety of books. Knowledge can be obtained throughout your daily living. Your focus in receiving the information is to be conscious of any activity you partake in. Ask questions to be curious about things surrounding you. Never assume you have all the answers. No one will ever have all the answers. People share information, some of it is true, and some information is not. Learn to decipher through facts and things that interest you. Do not limit yourself to whom you get the information from. Your brain is extremely powerful. Use it to the highest levels. Keep the brain sharp and remember as much information as possible.

BOREDOM

Believe it or not! You may just get bored in college. Your classes will keep you occupied a lot but what happens when you're ahead of schedule? Homework is done, studying is complete and you have time to enjoy the scenery, only you have nothing to do. What do you do? This is the moment when you take advantage of free time by creating things to do. Try treating yourself to the movies, it doesn't matter which movie you see, just pick one that looks interesting (you can never go wrong with an action pack film). Don't stop there! Indulge in a few snacks to heighten the moment. Even if you attend the theatre alone, make the best of it.

You could also attend student activities that are held on campus or head to an athletic event such as a basketball game or anything similar, if you're not interested in sports, go anyway, you never know, you may enjoy yourself. Another way to cure your boredom is playing stimulating brain puzzles like Sudoku. You could also grab a friend to hang out in the students lounge. If none of these are appealing, refer to the hobbies in the section (In case you become stressed) although, you are not stressed, these are extra ideas to help you with being bored.

Note: When your money is low or you just want to save, find free activities to do.

SHY STUDENTS

I once attended a competition in high school with my allied health class. We competed against many other schools. I was placed in a room for testing and later met up with my teacher and other students who attended and tested as well, only they were in different categories. We all sat in an auditorium, waiting for results of who had won in each category. I was so petrified of winning in my category. Why? I was afraid to walk a long distance to receive the award. All I could think was "there are so many people in here" and "what if I fall walking down these steps". I allowed these thoughts to crowd my mind to a point where I secretly didn't want to win because of my shyness.

There is nothing wrong with being shy. You will eventually grow out of your shell. In college, there will be times when you want to join clubs and participate in activities on campus or simply raise your hand in class to answer a question but then your timid ways kick in and you are unable to follow through with these tasks. Here are a few pointers to overcome shyness in college? First! You need confidence, so grab that pen and pad.

Write down all the good and positive things you like about yourself (nothing negative). Allow these words to marinate in your mind every day. You should read over these things daily and say them aloud. (Ex: I have a beautiful smile-I'm smart-I have a great personality) Why are you doing this? To remove any negative thoughts you have about yourself. You are placing focus on good things about yourself to become confident.

Secondly, get comfortable with things you say and do. Converse with yourself in the mirror for practice or use a video to record yourself talking, this way you can watch the video and see your facial expressions, body movements and listen to how you sound. The more practical you are, the better you become. If you're not great at communicating, it may take time but it can be done. If you do not like the way you look or sound on video, don't beat yourself up. Yes, we are our worst critics and we will dislike things about ourselves, however we need to accept our flaws and be content within ourselves, until there is self-improvement. No one will ever be perfect, but we can improve a lot in our lives. Third, get out of your comfort zone, talk to people daily, until it feels natural. Be open to different people and new things.

STEREOTYPING

Students are sometimes stereotyped in college by the way they look and things they like and even where they're from while this is unfair, it is true. It is not cool or acceptable to stereotype others, especially if you have never had a conversation with them or made any attempt to learn their ways and beliefs versus yours. This is college, this is the time to expand your knowledge and become open-minded. Instead of stereotyping, use your peer's differences to your advantage by exploring the diversity within the community rather than creating a negative atmosphere for them. You can learn new and interesting things about someone and maybe apply it elsewhere later in life or in your life today. For example, if you met a student from another country speaking a different language. Perhaps, you could get to know them and ask if they would teach you their language. If your major required a foreign language such as the one you're practicing, you will be ahead of schedule. You could also compare the differences of other students against yours and find that maybe you're not so different after all. Listen to others talk, pay close attention to how quickly labels are placed on one another. It's easy to stereotype but it's not easy being stereotyped.

STUDENTS WITH POTENTIAL

Potential wasn't granted to a select few students. You all have potential, the key to unlocking that potential resides within yourself. As a teenager, you may rely on your mother, father, sister or brother to say "it is possible for you to accomplish something" but the truth is support won't always be there. Not even from family. You must know you have potential and support yourself. Give yourself permission to do great things. Position yourself to turn that potential into reality. Try things that are out of your comfort zone. For example, you'll never know if you can play basketball if you don't try out for the team.

SELF CHALLENGE

Challenge yourself, march right into college, keeping in mind that you want the absolute best for yourself. Make a commitment to yourself that you will graduate with honors or make the dean's list. You don't have to broadcast it; this way you don't have to feel discouraged if things didn't go as planned. Remember, this is just a self-challenge and nothing to stress.

LET'S TALK ABOUT DRUGS

I know you've heard parents say don't do drugs, they may not explain in detail why you shouldn't. Basically, drugs affect your brain which is one of the most important parts in your body. Your brain sends a message to other parts of your body which allow it to take-in and respond to everything you experience. So, how important is your brain to you? How important is it for you to protect the one thing that controls you?

Drugs can become addictive and a bad habit. Any drug altering your thinking is harmful. Drugs are detrimental to your mind, body and overall life. Certain drugs make you look older than you really are. It also makes you behave in ways you cannot control. Experimenting with drugs mean you spend lots of money on these habits when this money could be put toward other items for college such as food, gas, or items for the dorm.

Note: Marijuana is legal in many states, however employers will not hire job seekers with this drug in their system.

COMPARISON

Have you ever compared yourself to someone else? Perhaps, a friend, classmate or maybe someone you just met. Comparing yourself isn't a good idea, many times it will affect the way you feel about yourself.

For example, let's say, you are in college and your grades are fair, you have a couple of friends. You're good with your life and the direction you're headed. At least until, you see an old classmate (from high school) whose grades are excellent and they appear to be popular with lots of friends. How do you feel comparing yourself to them? Are you suddenly dissatisfied with yourself?

If you are, you shouldn't be, your former classmate may not take as many credit hours as you. Meaning, they have more time to study, leading to better grades. Your old classmate may be more talkative and outgoing; their personality has attracted more friends. That doesn't mean the friendships you have are any less important. It doesn't mean you are any less important.

There are also those who compare themselves to people and feel superior because their car is a newer model or they appear to have more money or simply because their outer appearance is more fashionable. When someone compares their money, car, or external appearances to you or anyone else, it shows how insecure they are. There is always someone else who has more than them.

Once, they meet this person they too will feel inferior. So, it's best to stay away from the comparison chart. You can compare yourself to every person you meet but it doesn't change who you are or what you have. The best thing to do is be happy and satisfied with who you are. Don't compare yourself to anyone else; be thankful for all you have. It's great that you're able to attend college (even if it's not an elite college). It's great to have a car, regardless of the looks. It's wonderful to have a friend even if it's just one. You should only become better than you were yesterday.

HOW TO STAY MOTIVATED?

Staying motivated can be a challenge but with the right support group (family, friends, professors) you will keep going. In times when you're lacking motivation, think about the alternatives of not being in college. What would you do?

Remember that feeling in high school, walking across that stage with every one screaming your name, the big smiles from ear to ear, the feeling of knowing you never had to step foot back into the doors of high school. That feeling is maximized when receiving a college degree. Find motivation in music or poetry. You can search daily quotes to recite for encouragement. If there is a place of pain you never wish to return, think of it and use that as motivation to know you must never go back there again. Moving forward to complete college is your focus and you will follow through with it. Keep going, never give up.

Note: Meeting a peer with high energy and positive talk can also keep you motivated.

Tip: Join one club you find intriguing.

CREDIT CARDS

In addition to student loans, credit cards could either introduce you to debt, place you further in debt or it could be a wonderful tool of financial assistance. The decision is yours to make. The advantage of using credit cards is establishing credit, which can be done much later in life. If the credit card is used correctly, over a period, your credit score will increase, the higher the better. Correct use of the card will be paying the bill on time, and using it only when necessary. The disadvantage of using credit cards are high interest rates, an extra monthly bill you must re-pay even if you don't have the funds, if you are late making payments, it will ruin your credit score. If you are not employed or financially able to repay the credit card bill monthly, it is best not to use them. It is strongly suggested you talk with your parents before using credit cards in college.

DATING ON CAMPUS
SEXUAL TEMPTATION

Many students look to form relationships while on campus. Whether it is dating or platonic, both are desired. Laurie was at the top of her class in high school. Very intelligent young lady, she was awarded a full academic scholarship to a university. Making it to the end of her freshman year (still making good scores) she started dating a Sophomore in college. This guy was not as motivated or focused on grades as she was. He was more interested in partying and playing video games. He was doing barely enough in class for passing scores. Laurie dated this young man until her junior year. Unfortunately, around this time, Laurie learned she was pregnant and her grades began to drop because she was spending lots of time with him. Her grades dropped so low, they took the full academic scholarship, leaving her unable to pay for college. As a result, she was forced to quit with no financial assistance to return.

A relationship can be distracting if you are not dating someone who is like minded or determined as you are. As a young adult, away from home with no curfew and much freedom, you will be faced with lots of temptation and decisions.

The problem with sexual temptation is that it can interfere with your education. Before any sexual activities take place, stop and think about your future and what you want and do not want. This person you are tempted to be with, are you two serious about one another? If the answer is yes, make decisions to support one another by focusing on studies and doing what it takes to graduate successfully (together). Another thing to think about is kids, are you ready to be a parent? Pregnancy means you must prolong college. Do not allow any tempting situations to become a burden on your future life. Sex can wait. Stay focused on your education.

Your parents are not strangers. They want to help you with any problems you face. It may be uncomfortable to speak with them on this matter but they have experienced everything you may face in college (even if they didn't attend) they will have answers to your questions. If talking with your parents is not an option, talk with an older sibling, close friends or family members whom you'd consider a good role model. Just know that you are young and have so much time to experience relationships, love and anything else you may think about. Prioritize your life by putting yourself first and everything else will fall in place.

Note: There are many diseases that are spread among teenagers, many whom are unaware they are doing so.

WHEN CAMPUS
ACTIVITIES ARE TOO MUCH

As Mitchell sat in a class lecture with several students, he gazed at the clock and back down at his cell phone. He tapped his foot anxiously waiting for the lecture to end. "Alright read chapters five through eight over the weekend, test on Monday," the professor announced. That announcement went completely over his head. Mitchell only had one objective, get out of class and to the gym. Point guard on his team, one of the more popular guys on campus. He didn't feel it necessary to study because he was the star player and a asset to the team.

The following week, Mitchell got to class, took the test and failed horribly with an F. Of course, he wasn't worried until the professor spoke with him about his low scores on assignments and tests. The professor advised him that if he didn't get higher scores, he couldn't play sports. His scholarship would be taken away.

Mitchell panicked. He begged and pleaded with the professor to let him re-take the test. But the professor was very stubborn. He told Mitchell, "I've already done you a favor by bringing this to your attention." Mitchell called his coach, explained what was happening and with all three in a meeting. The professor finally gave in and said, "Mitchell has until the end of the week, he will be tested on Friday."

Sports, sororities and clubs are great activities however they are not priorities. Stressing about how you will ace a test and make it to practice is a lot of pressure. Times will get difficult in college but setting priorities is the best decision in this case.

Does your academic work come before football, basketball or any other sport? Yes, well don't be silent about the situation, talk with your coaches about your needs to see what alternatives are available. If they make light of your issue, be clear that receiving your degree is more important. After all, you must pass courses to stay in college. If you're not in college, you can't participate in athletics. So, stay focused on academics.

What about sororities? Or clubs? Talk with administrators and/or those leading these organizations. Again, your academic work is more important, you may have to set aside those activities to focus on passing courses. Lighten the load to be successful in your studies.

FITTING IN WITH PEERS

Are you one of those students that never found their place in high school? Do you feel you will be an outcast in college? Don't worry, everything will be okay. "Fitting in" is a problem for many teenagers and even still a problem for some adults. Finding your place in life or on campus can be a bit of a struggle. Everyone you encounter will not have the same interests, beliefs or backgrounds and for those reasons, students tend to gravitate toward people they have the most in common with. It's nothing against you, but hey, it's their loss, if only they knew that being around different people allows them to discover more great things about themselves. They'd do things differently. Fortunately, there is a cure for wanting to fit in and it may sound corny but the best cure is to "love who you are." Love everything about yourself from the way you wear your hair to the way you walk, talk, act or dress. Love it! Own it! Notice the great characteristics you have, accept the flaws. Fall in love with yourself. Become confident in how you approach life. Be confident in your spoken words as well as your appearance. Embrace the person in the mirror and as time passes, you'll learn things about yourself. Eventually, you will care less about mixing with the crowd. Fitting in will no longer be an issue because others will try to fit in with you. They will want to be in your presence. Love the beautiful being you are daily.

REASONS FOR ATTENDING COLLEGE

- *To become familiar with school administrators, make good scores and apply for a job within the college after graduation (good standing).*
- *To receive a recommendation letter from professors for job employment.*
- *To get away from your environment and position yourself to give back.*
- *You are intelligent and you can become whatever you want.*
- *Learn sign language (Check your area for specific schools).*
- *Development into a woman or man.*
- *To get on the college presidents list.*
- *You pick the college and teachers.*
- *To discipline yourself.*
- *To make you stronger.*
- *Overcome fear.*

PART 15

QUESTIONS

ARE YOU ATTENDING COLLEGE FOR YOURSELF OR OTHER PEOPLE?

There will be times when mom and dad wants us to attend college; not only do they persuade us to attend. Parents may even suggest which major to select. Other times, students follow the footsteps of the crowd, thinking college is the key to the future.

At some point, we must sit and think— "Am I heading to college for myself or others?" If attending college is your decision, you will have a willingness to complete assignments and be prompt for class. Chances are you will look forward to the experience and find it captivating.

Who is a better person to decide your future than you?

If you are attending college for other people you may not put as much effort into your studies. College is not for everyone and deciding not to continue does not mean you are a failure. It just means your skills are useful in other areas in life. However, always give college 100% effort before saying it is not for you.

Again, are you in college for yourself or someone else?

WHAT WERE YOUR GRADES IN HIGH SCHOOL? DO YOU WANT BETTER SCORES IN COLLEGE?

If you received low grades in high school, I doubt you want those same grades in college. What was the reason behind those low grades in high school? Were you not focused, were there problems at home to disturb your learning or were you just doing enough to get by? Are you proud of those grades, if not, you have another chance to excel and get those desired scores in college.

If you received high grades in high school, I know you would like to keep up the good work. Either way, college is waiting for you to take necessary steps in making acceptable scores. Be determined to reach your goal and pass the course.

DID YOU HAVE ANY REGRETS IN HIGH SCHOOL? IS IT POSSIBLE TO MAKE UP FOR ANY REGRETS OF THE PAST IN COLLEGE?

The biggest regret I have from high school is not playing basketball, the coach literally asked every day, "Would you join the team?"

I'd smile each time and say, "No."

"Why?"

"I don't want to." I'd say, but in my mind, I said, "yes! I want to play."

During these times, I was extremely shy! I had the height (still do) everything else would have come with practice. Had I just let go of the fear and played the game. I'm sure I would be playing professional sports today. If that's not enough torture, in college, a coach asked the exact same thing, unfortunately at this time, I thought it was too late for me and I said no once again.

Did you wish to participate in sports but was too shy to try out for the team? Now that you are in college, you could possibly talk to a coach and see if there are any options for joining the team. Do not miss a great opportunity as I did.

Are there any other regrets you had in high school? You could possibly wipe your slate clean and fix those regrets during college.

TOP TIPS TO KEEP IN MIND:

If you borrow a college loan and drop out, it still must be re-paid.

Repetition helps when studying.

If it is difficult to understand your professor, bring it to their attention immediately. If it doesn't get better, change professors (if possible). Not saying anything will affect you.

Be active in your college planning and be aware of your decisions

Check online before buying books at your college to save money.

Create index cards for a good study tool.

Not getting enough sleep interferes with your performance as a student. It decreases your ability to think and process information.

Have a list of questions to ask the admissions counselor prior to arrival.

Speak with the college counselor if you start having problems with your academic progress.

If you don't wish to engage in drinking alcoholic beverages but your friends insist, be stern in your decision not to do so.

Don't allow other college students that commute stay with you. You will get kicked off campus for breaking this rule. Depending on the college you can no longer return to the dorms.

Financial aid may not be available to students attending non-accredited colleges.

It's uncommon but some employers will require a certain GPA as a requirement. So, always do your best.

College advisors help students discover a career.

Keep in mind that every students experience will be different. For some students, college experiences will be challenging while for others, it will be a breeze. Academically, the level of difficulty depends on your major. If you are a student who wants to create a strong and positive foundation for his or her future, take full advantage of the opportunities your institution has to offer.

COLLEGE AFFIRMATIONS

Procrastination will not slow me down, today I will take action to get things done.

Some days are a little confusing but today I will prioritize, making my day easy and smooth.

Uncertainty pushes me back when I'm working to go forward, today I will have a clear vision on what's next.

Laziness holds me down and I refuse to be lazy. Today, I will get up and be prompt for class.

Incomplete assignments give me low scores. Today I will finish all assignments to get better scores.

It's so easy to give up and drop out but I will keep my focus and finish what I started.

Student loans are too high but after graduation, I have a six-month head start to repay my debt.

I really want to go home to be with family. Today I will call my family to fill the void of their absence.

I'm feeling lonely, so today I will find one person to hold a conversation with.

My classes are stressing me out. Today I will take it easy and slowly soak in information.

"No one else in my family even attended college, so I don't have to finish." Today, I will stop thinking this way and be the first college graduate in the family.

My classes are too difficult but I will find a tutor to help me understand the lesson.

OVERALL OBJECTIVE

The overall objective is choosing a major you're passionate about or choose something you enjoy doing every day. Ensure the major is high in demand for more job opportunities. Give yourself a limit of changing your major. If you begin the second major, complete it, there was a reason you chose it to begin with, right? Also, your major should gain profit and satisfaction.

Before choosing a college, decide which type of degree (Associate, Bachelors, Masters or Doctorate) is needed to complete the major and then choose the college type (community college, university or online college) that best fits your needs. Ensure these colleges are accredited. You can then narrow down what the colleges offer and where it's located. Check sources and carefully research for scholarships that may be available to you.

Mentally prepare yourself prior to meeting your roommate to be aware of what to expect from their personality and culture. Learn how to be direct with clear communication and no expectations of your dorm mate.

In class, learn that professors will allow you to be responsible for your own grades and work assignments. Participation in class helps you understand the lessons being taught. Students, it is possible to overcome discomfort in classrooms. Learn how to master your most difficult subject.

While you're socializing on campus, choose the crowd that could benefit you most. Be aware of the activities going on around you but also have fun and make friends in the process.

In college, try becoming a responsible leader. Find out who you are, if you can't seem to figure it out, do not worry, it will just take a little longer.

There are many objectives for this book. One is connecting you to the campus before you arrive. In doing so, I've introduced the peers, professors, classroom setting and campus fun. Another objective is making you aware of the decisions you make, on campus academically, financially, and socially. The main objective from the book is to guide students mentally and physically through their freshman year with more knowledge about college and their surrounding environment.

FINAL MESSAGE
TO STUDENTS

I support teenagers who want more from life. It's a headache to graduate high school and not know which direction to take. I encourage each student to make a move, whether it's furthering your education, going straight into the workforce or helping with a family business. The key is to be productive in whatever you decide.

At your age, the opportunities are endless but you must take chances to see what's out there for you. College may seem scary due to the expensive tuition, among other things, however it's possible to attend college with confidence. It's possible to have college success. The important reminder for college is to have a solid plan before making decisions.

My lack of guidance encouraged me to share my shortcomings and achievements throughout this book. When you're heading into college, always seek guidance. Gain as much insight as possible. My vow is to spread advice, tips, and experience with many students as possible. My wish is for each of you to exhaust all opportunities and complete college with no regrets.

Good luck to each of you!

REFERENCES:

bls.gov

www.fafsa.com

ABOUT THE AUTHOR

Felisha Upshaw, a graduate of Northwest Community College and a dedicated mentor to students of the Tennessee community. She founded the website www.collegenewbies.com (an online source for college freshman) which allow extensive support to students worldwide. Originally from Mississippi, currently resides in Memphis, TN.

Hello! Contact me with any questions about entering College. Don't be shy.

Website:
www.authorupshaw.com
www.collegenewbies.com

Social Networks:
Facebook: Facebook.com/AuthorUpshaw
Twitter: @CollegeNewbies

www.ingramcontent.com/pod-product-compliance
Lightning Source LLC
Chambersburg PA
CBHW031338040426
42443CB00006B/380